EASY EVERYDAY
dinners

EASY EVERYDAY
dinners

Go-to family recipes for each night of the week

by Kate Merker and the editors of *Woman's Day*

HEARST BOOKS
New York

Foreword

For many women, dinner is often a mad dash at the end of a long day. In my house I'm the cook, which means that I head straight for the stove right after I walk in the door. What works for me is simplicity—I have a short list of recipes with limited ingredients, quick cook time and only a few pots and pans (my husband, our household's chief dishwashing officer, is appreciative). I plan meals ahead, shop weekly for ingredients, and try to make a freezable soup or stew over the weekend. Finally, I always order pizza on Friday night—even the best cooks need a break!

My approach reflects what *Woman's Day* is all about. Our Easy Everyday column—one of the magazine's most popular sections—makes it simple to get a fresh and healthy meal on the table without a major time commitment, a bank loan for exotic ingredients or a dozen trips to the supermarket. The recipes, developed by Food and Nutrition Director Kate Merker and her crackerjack team, are guaranteed family pleasers.

We've gathered our most popular dinner recipes from Easy Everyday into this cookbook. Think of it as your go-to, your timesaver, your problem solver, your cooking buddy. The recipes will quickly become part of your own rotation, which means less time cooking and more time enjoying.

Susan

Susan Spencer
EDITOR-IN-CHIEF, *WOMAN'S DAY*

Introduction

Ask any reader, past or present, what she loves most about *Woman's Day*, and she'll say without the slightest hesitation, "The recipes!" For 76 years the WD food editors have been steaming, sautéing, stir-frying, broiling and braising to create recipes that are simple, delicious and fast. Our kitchen looks a lot like yours: We have a regular stove and oven, a beat-up but beloved stand mixer and a seasoned 6-qt slow cooker. We cook like you do, except we put our recipes through a long and rigorous process of testing and tweaking until we're 100% happy. We take pride in our recipes so that you can be proud of the meals you serve your family.

Good and Good for You

As we develop recipes for each issue, nutrition is front of mind—we keep an eye on calorie and sodium counts, and we've never met a vegetable we didn't like. But we also believe that mixing in some savory (or sweet!) indulgences into a week of healthy dinners keeps everyone happy and satisfied. So you can make wise choices, each recipe in this cookbook includes nutritional information. We also added a ♥ icon for every recipe that meets our heart-healthy criteria and noted some of those that come in at 400 calories or less.

Pennywise, Not Pound Foolish

Getting dinner on the table shouldn't break the bank. Just as we do in the magazine, we've priced out each recipe in this cookbook so you know how much it will run you per serving. To determine costs we used a combination of national averages from the United States Department of Agriculture (USDA), grocery store prices from around the country and the suggested retail price of nationally available brands for packaged, canned and frozen ingredients. It's not an exact science—as a careful shopper, you know that grocery prices change frequently depending on what's on sale and where you shop—but using this information as a guideline will help you make informed choices that benefit your wallet.

Eating with Joy

Cooking is one of the great joys in life, and it is our hope that these recipes will bring you as much pleasure as they have us. From our kitchen to yours, the editors at *Woman's Day* wish you many delicious meals with your family and friends.

Happy cooking,

Kate

Kate Merker
FOOD & NUTRITION DIRECTOR, *WOMAN'S DAY*

p25

p26

p28

Poultry

p29

p30

p32

SLOW COOKER

Spring chicken stew

ACTIVE 15 MIN • **TOTAL** 4 HR 15 MIN OR 6 HR 15 MIN • **SERVES** 4
COST PER SERVING $2.29

½	cup dry white wine
2	Tbsp all-purpose flour
	Kosher salt and pepper
4	medium carrots, peeled and cut into 1-in. pieces
2	stalks celery, sliced ¼ in. thick
1	medium onion, chopped
2	lb boneless, skinless chicken thighs, trimmed and cut into 2-in. pieces
8	oz egg noodles
2	Tbsp olive oil
2	Tbsp Dijon mustard
1	Tbsp fresh tarragon, roughly chopped, plus more for serving
1	cup frozen peas

1 In a 5- to 6-qt slow cooker, whisk together the wine, flour, ½ cup water and ½ tsp each salt and pepper.

2 Add the carrots, celery, onion and chicken and toss to combine. Cook, covered, until the chicken is cooked through and easily pulls apart, 5 to 6 hours on low or 3 to 4 hours on high.

3 Twenty-five minutes before serving, prepare the noodles according to package directions. Reserve ¼ cup of the cooking liquid, drain the noodles and return them to the pot. Add the oil, mustard, 2 Tbsp of the reserved water and ¼ tsp each salt and pepper and toss to coat (adding more water if the pasta seems dry). Toss with the tarragon.

4 Gently fold the peas into the stew and cook, covered, until heated through, about 2 minutes. Serve over the noodles and sprinkle with additional tarragon, if desired.

PER SERVING 619 cal, 19 g fat (4 g sat fat), 228 mg chol, 819 mg sod, 54 g pro, 55 g car, 6 g fiber

Switch it up » For an easy pot pie, omit the pasta. Prepare 1 can refrigerated biscuits (such as Pillsbury Flaky Golden Layers) according to package directions, topping each with 1 Tbsp grated Cheddar before baking. Stir the tarragon through the stew; spoon into bowls, then top with the cheesy biscuits.

EASY ENTERTAINING

Balsamic chicken with apple, lentil and spinach salad

ACTIVE 15 MIN • **TOTAL** 25 MIN • **SERVES** 4
COST PER SERVING $1.90

3   Tbsp olive oil

4   6-oz boneless,
    skinless chicken breasts

    Kosher salt and pepper

2   Tbsp balsamic vinegar

2   scallions, thinly sliced

1   green apple,
    cut into small pieces

1   stalk celery, thinly sliced

2   Tbsp fresh lemon juice

1   15-oz can lentils, rinsed

2   cups baby spinach, chopped

½   cup fresh flat-leaf parsley,
    roughly chopped

❶ Heat 1 Tbsp oil in a large skillet over medium heat. Season the chicken with ½ tsp each salt and pepper and cook until golden brown and cooked through, 8 to 10 minutes per side. Remove from heat, add the vinegar and turn the chicken to coat.

❷ Meanwhile, in a large bowl, toss the scallions, apple, celery, lemon juice, remaining 2 Tbsp oil, ½ tsp salt and ¼ tsp pepper. Fold in the lentils, spinach and parsley. Serve with the chicken.

♥ PER SERVING 394 cal, 13 g fat (1 g sat fat), 95 mg chol, 755 mg sod, 46 g pro, 25 g car, 10 g fiber

Switch it up » Try this dish with boneless pork chops instead of chicken. Cook the pork chops until golden brown and just cooked through, 6 to 8 minutes per side.

Chicken paprikash

ACTIVE 30 MIN • **TOTAL** 30 MIN
SERVES 4

COST PER SERVING $2.00

8	oz wide egg noodles
½	cup fresh flat-leaf parsley, chopped
2	Tbsp olive oil
1½	lb boneless, skinless chicken breasts, cut into 2½-in. pieces
	Kosher salt and pepper
½	cup dry white wine
1	large onion, sliced
1	green bell pepper, sliced
2	cloves garlic, chopped
1	28-oz can whole peeled tomatoes
1	Tbsp paprika
½	cup sour cream

❶ Cook the egg noodles according to package directions. Drain and return to the pot. Toss with the parsley.

❷ Meanwhile, heat 1 Tbsp oil in a large skillet over medium-high heat. Season the chicken with ½ tsp salt and ¼ tsp pepper and cook until browned, 2 to 3 minutes per side. Transfer to a bowl. Add the wine to the skillet and cook, scraping up any brown bits, for 2 minutes. Transfer to the bowl with the chicken.

❸ Wipe out the skillet and heat the remaining Tbsp oil over medium heat. Add the onion, bell pepper and garlic and cook, stirring occasionally, until tender, 5 to 6 minutes.

❹ Crush the tomatoes and add them (and their juices) to the skillet, along with the paprika, ½ tsp salt and ¼ tsp pepper. Add the chicken and any juices, nestling the chicken in the mixture. Simmer until the chicken is cooked through, 2 to 3 minutes. Remove from heat and stir in the sour cream. Serve with the noodles.

Use up the sour cream » Make a quick baked potato topping: Combine ½ cup sour cream, ¼ cup grated Cheddar, 2 finely chopped scallions, 1 Tbsp chopped parsley and 2 tsp paprika.

PER SERVING 507 cal, 16 g fat (5 g sat fat), 140 mg chol, 1,055 mg sod, 47 g pro, 43 g car, 5 g fiber

FAMILY FAVORITE

Jerk chicken with beans and rice

ACTIVE 25 MIN • **TOTAL** 35 MIN • **SERVES** 4

COST PER SERVING $1.55

8   small chicken drumsticks
    (about 2½ lb total)

2   Tbsp fresh lime juice

3   Tbsp olive oil

2   Tbsp dry jerk seasoning

1   large onion, chopped

    Kosher salt and pepper

2   cloves garlic, finely chopped

1   cup long-grain white rice

2   cups low-sodium chicken broth

1   15-oz can kidney beans, rinsed

2   scallions, thinly sliced

❶ Heat oven to 400°F. On a rimmed baking sheet, toss the chicken with the lime juice and 1 Tbsp oil, then sprinkle with the jerk seasoning. Roast until the chicken is cooked through, 25 to 30 minutes.

❷ Meanwhile, heat the remaining 2 Tbsp oil in a medium saucepan over medium heat. Add the onion, season with ½ tsp salt and ¼ tsp pepper and cook, covered, stirring occasionally, for 5 minutes. Stir in the garlic and cook for 1 minute.

❸ Stir in the rice, then add the broth and bring to a boil. Reduce heat and simmer, covered, until the rice is tender and the liquid is absorbed, 15 to 18 minutes; fluff with a fork. Fold in the beans and cook until heated through, about 2 minutes. Fold in the scallions and serve with the chicken.

PER SERVING 659 cal, 23 g fat (5 g sat fat), 97 mg chol, 1,000 mg sod, 42 g pro, 69 g car, 11 g fiber

Use up the jerk seasoning » This spice mix adds an exotic flavor to oven-baked fries. Toss sliced potatoes or sweet potatoes with olive oil and jerk seasoning and roast at 400°F until golden brown and tender, 30 to 35 minutes.

5-INGREDIENT MEAL*

Crispy chicken with roasted Brussels sprouts and red onions

ACTIVE 20 MIN • **TOTAL** 30 MIN • **SERVES** 4
COST PER SERVING $1.93

1   lb small Brussels sprouts,
    halved (quartered, if large)

1   large red onion,
    cut into ½-in. wedges

3   Tbsp olive oil
    Kosher salt and pepper

8   small chicken thighs
    (2 lb total)

8   cloves garlic, smashed

2   sprigs fresh rosemary,
    broken into small pieces

* We consider olive oil, salt and pepper to
  be staples, so they are not included in the
  ingredient count for this recipe.

① Heat oven to 425°F. On a large rimmed baking sheet, toss the Brussels sprouts, onion, 2 Tbsp oil, ½ tsp salt and ¼ tsp pepper. Roast until golden brown and tender, 20 to 25 minutes.

② Meanwhile, heat the remaining Tbsp oil in a large skillet over medium heat. Season the chicken with ½ tsp each salt and pepper and cook, skin-side down, until the skin is crisp, 7 to 8 minutes.

③ Turn the chicken, add the garlic and rosemary to the pan, and cook until the garlic is golden brown and the chicken is cooked through, 5 to 6 minutes more. Serve with the vegetables.

PER SERVING 461 cal, 29 g fat (6 g sat fat), 112 mg chol, 615 mg sod, 35 g pro, 16 g car, 5 g fiber

Prep tip » Look for Brussels sprouts that are no more than an inch in diameter (larger ones taste too cabbagey) and have firm, compact bright green heads.

Cool chicken and noodle salad

ACTIVE 20 MIN • **TOTAL** 20 MIN • **SERVES** 4

COST PER SERVING $2.36

8	oz angel hair or capellini pasta
1	Tbsp toasted sesame oil (optional)
¼	cup fresh lime juice
2	Tbsp light brown sugar
1	red chile, thinly sliced or ½ tsp crushed red pepper flakes
	Kosher salt and pepper
1	Granny Smith apple, cut into wedges and thinly sliced
½	seedless cucumber, cut into thin half-moons
2	scallions, thinly sliced
1	2- to 2½-lb rotisserie chicken
¼	cup fresh mint, thinly sliced

❶ Cook the noodles according to package directions. Rinse under cold water to cool, then toss with the sesame oil (if using).

❷ Meanwhile, in a large bowl, whisk together the lime juice, brown sugar, chile, ½ tsp salt and ¼ tsp pepper. Add the apple, cucumber and scallions to the lime juice mixture and toss to coat.

❸ Slice or shred the chicken, discarding the bones. Add to the apple-cucumber mixture and toss to combine, then toss with the noodles and mint.

PER SERVING 542 cal, 12 g fat (3 g sat fat), 126 mg chol, 743 mg sod, 49 g pro, 57 g car, 3 g fiber

ONE-POT

Spanish-style chicken and rice

ACTIVE 20 MIN • **TOTAL** 35 MIN • **SERVES** 4

COST PER SERVING $1.80

1	Tbsp olive oil
1½	lb boneless, skinless chicken breasts, cut into 3-in. pieces
	Kosher salt and pepper
1	medium onion, thinly sliced
1	green bell pepper, thinly sliced
2	cloves garlic, thinly sliced
2	14.5-oz cans diced tomatoes with chiles (such as Del Monte, Hunt's or Ro*Tel)
¾	cup long-grain white rice
½	cup fresh flat-leaf parsley, chopped
¼	cup pimiento-stuffed olives, chopped (optional)

Switch it up » Turn this tasty one-pot meal into a quick paella by adding ½ lb raw shrimp and 1 cup frozen peas during the last 4 minutes of cooking.

❶ Heat the oil in a large skillet over medium-high heat. Season the chicken with ¼ tsp each salt and pepper and cook on one side until golden brown, about 3 minutes.

❷ Turn the chicken, moving it to the outsides of the skillet. Add the onion, bell pepper and garlic and cook, stirring occasionally, for 5 minutes.

❸ Add the tomatoes (and their juices) and 1 cup water to the skillet, then stir in the rice. Simmer, covered, until the rice is tender, 18 to 20 minutes. Sprinkle with the parsley and olives (if using).

♥ **PER SERVING** 411 cal, 7 g fat (2 g sat fat), 95 mg chol, 678 mg sod, 42 g pro, 45 g car, 4 g fiber

ONE-POT

Quick sausage, white bean and spinach stew

ACTIVE 15 MIN • **TOTAL** 30 MIN • **SERVES** 4
COST PER SERVING $3.51

1	Tbsp olive oil
12	oz fully cooked Italian chicken sausage, sliced ¼ in. thick
4	cloves garlic, thinly sliced
½	cup dry white wine
1	32-oz container low-sodium chicken broth
4	oz ditalini pasta or other soup pasta (about 1 cup)
1	15.5-oz can cannellini or other white beans, rinsed
	Black pepper
1	10-oz bag spinach, thick stems removed
1	oz Parmesan, grated (about ¼ cup)

1 Heat the oil in a large saucepan over medium heat. Add the sausage and cook, stirring occasionally, until browned, 4 to 5 minutes. Using a slotted spoon, transfer the sausage to a plate.

2 Add the garlic to the pan and cook, stirring, for 1 minute (do not let it brown). Add the wine and simmer, scraping up any brown bits, for 1 minute.

3 Add the broth and pasta and bring to a boil. Reduce heat and simmer until the pasta is just tender, 8 to 10 minutes.

4 Add the beans, sausage and ¼ tsp pepper and cook until heated through, about 2 minutes. Remove from heat and add the spinach, stirring gently until it begins to wilt. Serve with the Parmesan.

PER SERVING 429 cal, 15 g fat (4 g sat fat), 76 mg chol, 1,188 mg sod, 30 g pro, 42 g car, 6 g fiber

Make ahead » Refrigerate the stew for up to 3 days. Reheat in a medium saucepan, covered, stirring occasionally.

Quick turkey chili

ACTIVE 25 MIN • **TOTAL** 25 MIN • **SERVES** 6

COST PER SERVING $2.04

2	Tbsp olive oil
1	large onion, chopped
	Kosher salt and pepper
2	cloves garlic, finely chopped
1	Tbsp chili powder
2	tsp ground cumin
1¼	lb lean ground turkey
1	28-oz can fire-roasted diced tomatoes
1	15-oz can refried beans
1	15-oz can black beans, rinsed
1	15-oz can kidney beans, rinsed
2	4-oz cans fire-roasted diced chiles, drained
1	cup low-sodium chicken broth
	Sour cream, grated cheese and tortilla chips, for serving

Make ahead » Freeze the chili for up to 3 months. Thaw in the refrigerator overnight, then reheat in a medium saucepan, covered, stirring occasionally (add ½ cup water or chicken broth if the chili seems too thick).

❶ Heat the oil in a large saucepan or Dutch oven over medium heat. Add the onion, season with ½ tsp each salt and pepper and cook, covered, stirring occasionally, until tender, 6 to 8 minutes.

❷ Stir in the garlic, chili powder and cumin and cook, stirring, for 1 minute. Add the turkey and cook, breaking it up with a spoon, until it begins to brown, about 4 minutes.

❸ Add the tomatoes (and their juices), beans, chiles and chicken broth and bring to a boil. Reduce heat and simmer until slightly thickened, about 3 minutes. Serve with the sour cream, cheese and chips, if desired.

PER SERVING 446 cal, 12 g fat (3 g sat fat), 54 mg chol, 1,186 mg sod, 35 g pro, 51 g car, 17 g fiber

EASY ENTERTAINING

Brick chicken with garlic and thyme

ACTIVE 10 MIN • **TOTAL** 25 MIN • **SERVES** 4
COST PER SERVING $1.49

8	small chicken thighs (2 lb total)
8	cloves garlic (in their skins), smashed
8	sprigs fresh thyme
1	Tbsp olive oil
¼	to ½ tsp crushed red pepper flakes
	Kosher salt
	Cooked green beans, for serving

1 In a large bowl, toss the chicken, garlic, thyme, oil, crushed red pepper and ½ tsp salt.

2 Heat a 12-in. cast-iron skillet over medium heat until hot, about 2 minutes. Place chicken, skin-side down, in the skillet and spoon the garlic and thyme mixture around it. Place a second skillet on top of the chicken and put heavy cans in the skillet to weigh it down (this will flatten the chicken so it cooks up evenly and extra crisp). Cook for 10 minutes.

3 Remove the cans and top skillet, turn chicken over and stir the garlic. Return the skillet and cans and cook until the chicken is crisp and cooked through, 5 to 6 minutes more. Serve with green beans, if desired.

PER SERVING 366 cal, 25 g fat (7 g sat fat), 115 mg chol, 343 mg sod, 31 g pro, 2 g car, 0 g fiber

Cook's tip » If seasoned regularly, your cast-iron skillet can last for decades and turn out flapjacks for generations to come. Go to *womansday.com/skillet* for a how-to.

SLOW COOKER

Chicken Marbella

ACTIVE 15 MIN • **TOTAL** 3 TO 4 HR ON HIGH OR 5 TO 6 HR ON LOW • **SERVES** 4
COST PER SERVING $1.61

½   cup white wine

2   Tbsp brown sugar

1½ tsp dried oregano

3   Tbsp red wine vinegar
    Kosher salt and pepper

6   cloves garlic, smashed

1   Tbsp capers

½   cup prunes

¼   cup pitted green olives

4   small chicken legs, split
    (4 drumsticks, 4 thighs; about
    2½ lb total), skin removed

1   cup long-grain white rice

¼   cup fresh flat-leaf parsley,
    chopped

❶ In a 5- to 6-qt slow cooker, whisk together the wine, brown sugar, oregano, 2 Tbsp vinegar, and ¼ tsp each salt and pepper. Add the garlic, capers, prunes and olives and mix to combine.

❷ Add the chicken, nestling it among the olives and prunes. Cover and cook until the meat is tender and cooked through, on low for 5 to 6 hours or on high for 3 to 4 hours.

❸ Thirty minutes before serving, cook the rice according to package directions. Gently stir in the remaining Tbsp vinegar and parsley into the chicken mixture. Serve the chicken, prunes, olives and cooking liquid over the rice.

PER SERVING 302 cal, 8 g fat (2 g sat fat), 129 mg chol, 487 mg sod, 34 g pro, 24 g car, 2 g fiber

Switch it up » Although prunes are standard in Marbella recipes, try swapping them out for dried apricots or nectarines. If using nectarines, cut them into 1-in. pieces before adding them to the slow cooker.

Gumbo

ACTIVE 25 MIN • **TOTAL** 30 MIN • **SERVES** 4

COST PER SERVING $2.48

1 cup long-grain white rice	Kosher salt and pepper
1 Tbsp olive oil	¼ cup all-purpose flour
1 12- to 14-oz pkg kielbasa, cut into ¼-in. slices	¼ tsp ground allspice
	¼ to ½ tsp cayenne
1 lb boneless, skinless chicken thighs, cut into 1½-in. pieces	1 14.5-oz can low-sodium chicken broth
1 large onion, chopped	1 14.5-oz can diced tomatoes
4 stalks celery, chopped	4 sprigs fresh thyme
1 large green bell pepper, chopped	½ 16-oz bag frozen sliced okra

1 Cook the rice according to package directions.

2 Meanwhile, heat the oil in a large pot over medium-high heat. Add the kielbasa and cook, stirring once, until slightly browned, 2 to 3 minutes; transfer to a large bowl. Add the chicken to the pot and cook, stirring, until browned, 2 to 3 minutes; transfer to the bowl with the kielbasa.

3 Add the onion, celery, green bell pepper and ¼ tsp each salt and pepper and cook, covered, stirring occasionally, until just tender, 6 to 8 minutes. Sprinkle the flour, allspice and cayenne over the vegetables. Cook, stirring constantly, until onion begins to brown, 1 to 2 minutes.

4 Add the broth, tomatoes (and their juices) and thyme and bring to a simmer. Stir in the okra, kielbasa and chicken and cook until the okra is tender and mixture is slightly thickened, 5 to 6 minutes. Serve with the rice.

Make ahead » Refrigerate the gumbo for up to 2 days. Reheat in a large saucepan, covered, stirring occasionally.

PER SERVING 672 cal, 25 g fat (8 g sat fat), 160 mg chol, 1,677 mg sod, 43 g pro, 67 g car, 5 g fiber

UNDER 400 CALORIES

Seared chicken with creamy spinach and artichokes

ACTIVE 25 MIN • **TOTAL** 25 MIN • **SERVES** 4
COST PER SERVING $1.92

- 2 Tbsp olive oil
- 4 6-oz boneless, skinless chicken breasts
  Kosher salt and pepper
- 1 lemon, halved
- 1 14-oz can artichoke hearts, halved
- 2 cloves garlic, thinly sliced
- ½ cup dry white wine
- ¼ cup lowfat sour cream
- 1 bunch spinach, thick stems discarded

❶ Heat 1 Tbsp oil in a large skillet over medium heat. Season the chicken with ½ tsp each salt and pepper and cook until golden brown, 5 to 6 minutes.

❷ Turn the chicken, place the lemon in the skillet cut-side down, and continue cooking until the chicken is cooked through, 5 to 6 minutes more. Squeeze the juice of the cooked lemon halves all over the chicken.

❸ While the chicken is cooking, heat the remaining Tbsp oil in a second skillet over medium-high heat. Add the artichokes, cut-side down, and cook until golden brown, about 3 minutes. Reduce heat to medium, add the garlic and cook, tossing, until golden brown, about 2 minutes.

❹ Stir in the wine and cook for 2 minutes. Stir in the sour cream. Add the spinach, season with ¼ tsp each salt and pepper and cook, tossing gently, until the spinach begins to wilt, 1 to 2 minutes. Serve with the chicken.

Switch it up » This creamy spinach and artichoke side is also a great accompaniment to seared fish or tossed with pasta for a vegetarian main course.

PER SERVING 298 cal, 10 g fat (2 g sat fat), 95 mg chol, 689 mg sod, 39 g pro, 11 g car, 2 g fiber

FAMILY FAVORITE

Spice-roasted chicken, red onions, carrots and parsnips

ACTIVE 15 MIN • **TOTAL** 50 MIN • **SERVES** 4
COST PER SERVING $1.83

2	medium red onions, cut into ½-in. wedges
1½	lb medium carrots, cut into 3-in. sticks
½	lb medium parsnips, cut into 3-in. sticks
2	Tbsp olive oil
	Kosher salt and pepper
4	small chicken legs, split (4 thighs, 4 drumsticks)
2	tsp paprika
1	tsp ground cinnamon

1 Heat oven to 425°F. On a large rimmed baking sheet, toss the onions, carrots, parsnips, oil and ¼ tsp each salt and pepper. Transfer half of the vegetables to a second large baking sheet.

2 Season the chicken with the paprika, cinnamon, ½ tsp salt and ¼ tsp pepper. Nestle the chicken pieces among the vegetables and roast for 15 minutes. Switch the positions of the baking sheets and roast until the chicken is cooked through and the vegetables are golden brown and tender, 15 to 20 minutes more.

PER SERVING 386 cal, 23 g fat (5 g sat fat), 105 mg chol, 574 mg sod, 32 g pro, 30 g car, 8 g fiber

Switch it up » Add more types of vegetables to this dish. Use half the amount of carrots and substitute halved new potatoes, turnip wedges, small pieces of rutabaga or a combination.

FAMILY FAVORITE

Crispy chicken salad with buttermilk blue cheese dressing

ACTIVE 15 MIN • **TOTAL** 25 MIN • **SERVES** 4
COST PER SERVING $1.95

4	cups corn flakes, crushed
½	cup buttermilk
4	6-oz boneless, skinless chicken breasts
¼	tsp cayenne pepper
	Kosher salt and pepper
¼	cup sour cream
1	Tbsp white wine vinegar
½	cup blue cheese, crumbled (about 2 oz), plus more for serving
2	Tbsp chopped fresh chives
1	head iceberg lettuce, cut into 4 wedges
1	cup cherry or grape tomatoes, sliced

① Heat oven to 400°F. Line a rimmed baking sheet with nonstick foil. Place the corn flakes in a shallow bowl.

② Using ¼ cup of the buttermilk, brush the chicken breasts on all sides, then season with the cayenne, ½ tsp salt and ¼ tsp pepper. Coat the chicken in the corn flakes, pressing gently to help them adhere, and place on the prepared baking sheet. Bake until cooked through, 15 to 20 minutes.

③ Meanwhile, make the dressing: In a medium bowl, whisk together the sour cream, vinegar and remaining ¼ cup buttermilk. Stir in the blue cheese and 1 Tbsp chives.

④ Divide the lettuce and tomatoes among plates. Spoon the dressing over the top. Sprinkle with the remaining Tbsp chives and additional blue cheese, if desired. Serve with the chicken.

PER SERVING 422 cal, 13 g fat (7 g sat fat), 117 mg chol, 879 mg sod, 44 g pro, 33 g car, 3 g fiber

Love your leftovers » Cut leftover chicken into 1-in. pieces and chop any leftover lettuce. Wrap in large flour tortillas and serve with hot sauce for a Buffalo wing-inspired lunch.

p49

p50

p52

Beef & Lamb

p53

p54

p56

FAMILY FAVORITE

Balsamic meat loaf with garlicky beans and greens

ACTIVE 20 MIN • **TOTAL** 40 MIN • **SERVES** 4

COST PER SERVING $2.16

¼	cup plus 2 Tbsp ketchup
4	Tbsp balsamic vinegar
2	large eggs
	Kosher salt and pepper
½	cup dry bread crumbs
6	cloves garlic (4 finely chopped, 2 thinly sliced)
1	cup fresh flat-leaf parsley, chopped
1½	lb lean ground beef
2	Tbsp olive oil
¼	to ½ tsp crushed red pepper flakes (optional)
1	15.5-oz can cannellini beans, rinsed
1	bunch spinach, thick stems discarded (5 oz)

❶ Heat oven to 375°F. Line a rimmed baking sheet with foil. In a small bowl, whisk together ¼ cup ketchup and 2 Tbsp vinegar; set aside.

❷ In a large bowl, whisk together the eggs, remaining 2 Tbsp ketchup and vinegar, ¾ tsp salt and ½ tsp pepper; stir in the bread crumbs. Mix in the chopped garlic and parsley. Add the beef and mix just until incorporated.

❸ Divide the mixture into four portions, transfer to the prepared baking sheet and shape into 4½ x 3-in. loaves. Bake for 15 minutes. Brush with the ketchup-vinegar mixture and bake until the internal temperature reaches 150°F, 5 to 10 minutes more. Let rest for 5 minutes before slicing.

❹ While the meat loaves rest, heat the oil in a large skillet over medium heat. Add the sliced garlic and crushed red pepper (if using) and cook, stirring, until golden brown, 2 minutes. Add the beans and ¼ cup water and cook until heated through, about 3 minutes. Add the spinach, season with ½ tsp salt and ¼ tsp pepper and cook, tossing, until spinach begins to wilt, 1 to 2 minutes. Serve with the meat loaves.

PER SERVING 464 cal, 24 g fat (7 g sat fat), 197 mg chol, 1,102 mg sod, 39 g pro, 22 g car, 2 g fiber

Make ahead » Divide the raw meat mixture among 4 pieces of foil and shape into loaves. Wrap each in plastic and freeze in a resealable bag for up to 3 months. Thaw in the refrigerator overnight. Unwrap and place the loaves on a foil-lined baking sheet. Bake and glaze as directed.

15 MINUTE MEAL

Chili steak with tomato and jalapeño salad

ACTIVE 15 MIN • **TOTAL** 15 MIN • **SERVES** 4
COST PER SERVING $3.62

1½ lb skirt steak, cut into 4 pieces

1 tsp chili powder

Kosher salt and pepper

1½ lb plum tomatoes, cut into 1-in. pieces

2 scallions, thinly sliced

1 jalapeño (seeded for less heat, if desired), thinly sliced

1 small clove garlic, finely chopped

2 Tbsp lime juice

1 cup fresh cilantro, chopped

Small flour tortillas, for serving

❶ Heat broiler. Line a broiler-proof rimmed baking sheet with foil. Season the steak with the chili powder and ½ tsp each salt and pepper. Place on the baking sheet and broil to desired doneness, 3 to 4 minutes per side for medium-rare. Transfer to a cutting board and let rest for at least 5 minutes before slicing.

❷ Meanwhile, in a medium bowl, toss together the tomatoes, scallions, jalapeño, garlic, lime juice, ½ tsp salt and ¼ tsp pepper. Fold in the cilantro. Serve with the steak and tortillas, if desired.

PER SERVING 319 cal, 16 g fat (6 g sat fat), 77 mg chol, 600 mg sod, 35 g pro, 8 g car, 3 g fiber

Easy side » Make quick quesadillas: Sprinkle shredded Muenster cheese or Cheddar cheese on one side of each tortilla. Fold the other side over the cheese and broil until golden brown and crisp, 1 to 2 minutes per side.

Sweet potato, kielbasa and red onion pizza

ACTIVE 10 MIN • **TOTAL** 35 MIN • **SERVES** 4
COST PER SERVING $1.63

Cornmeal, for the baking sheet

1 lb pizza dough (thawed, if frozen)

1 medium sweet potato (or about 8 oz of another potato), peeled and cut into thin half-moons

1 medium red onion, thinly sliced

1 Tbsp olive oil

Kosher salt and pepper

6 oz beef, pork or turkey kielbasa (or fully cooked chicken sausage)

6 oz sharp Cheddar or other cheese, grated (about 1½ cups)

2 Tbsp Dijon mustard

❶ Heat oven to 425°F. Dust a baking sheet with cornmeal (or coat with oil if you do not have cornmeal). Shape the dough into a 16-in. circle, oval or rectangle and place on the prepared baking sheet.

❷ In a large bowl, toss the potato, onion, oil, ¼ tsp salt and ½ tsp pepper. Add the kielbasa and cheese and toss to combine.

❸ Spread the mustard on the dough, leaving a ½-in. border all the way around. Scatter the vegetable-kielbasa mixture over the dough and bake until the potatoes are tender and the crust is golden brown and crisp, 20 to 25 minutes. Serve with a salad, if desired.

Make ahead » Refrigerate the cooked pizza for up to 2 days. When ready to serve, bake at 375°F until heated through.

PER SERVING 620 cal, 27 g fat (12 g sat fat), 68 mg chol, 1,675 mg sod, 26 g pro, 68 g car, 2 g fiber

UNDER 400 CALORIES

Steak and noodle salad

ACTIVE 25 MIN • **TOTAL** 25 MIN • **SERVES** 4
COST PER SERVING $2.36

4	oz rice noodles
2	Tbsp rice vinegar
2	Tbsp olive oil
½	lb flank steak
	Kosher salt and pepper
4	oz shiitake mushrooms, stems discarded, caps sliced
4	oz snow peas, thinly sliced lengthwise
2	cloves garlic, finely chopped
1	red chile, thinly sliced
1	Tbsp finely chopped fresh ginger
½	cup fresh cilantro

❶ Cook the noodles according to package directions. Drain and rinse under cold water to cool; transfer to a large bowl and toss with the rice vinegar.

❷ Heat 1 Tbsp of the oil in a large skillet over medium-high heat. Season the steak with ¼ tsp each salt and pepper, and cook to desired doneness, 3 to 5 minutes per side for medium-rare. Transfer to a cutting board and let rest for 5 minutes before slicing.

❸ Wipe out the skillet and heat the remaining Tbsp oil over medium-high heat. Add the mushrooms and cook, tossing occasionally, for 3 minutes. Add the snow peas, garlic, chile, ginger and ¼ tsp each salt and pepper, and cook, tossing, until the snow peas are just tender, 2 to 3 minutes.

❹ Toss the noodles with the vegetables, cilantro and steak.

♥ **PER SERVING** 345 cal, 12 g fat (4 g sat fat), 38 mg chol, 296 mg sod, 25 g pro, 33 g car, 2 g fiber

Prep tip » Tightly wrapped fresh ginger will keep in the freezer for up to 3 months and can be grated or sliced frozen—no need to thaw it.

FAMILY FAVORITE

Barbecue beef and mashed potato pie

ACTIVE 25 MIN • **TOTAL** 30 MIN • **SERVES** 6
COST PER SERVING $1.37

2 lb Yukon gold or white potatoes, peeled and cut into 2-in. pieces

Kosher salt and pepper

4 Tbsp olive oil

1 large onion, chopped

1½ lb lean ground beef

4 plum tomatoes, seeded and diced

½ cup ketchup

2 Tbsp cider vinegar

1 Tbsp Dijon mustard

1 Tbsp molasses

1 Tbsp Worcestershire sauce

❶ Place the potatoes in a pot. Add cold water to cover; bring to a boil. Add 1 tsp salt; simmer until just tender, 15 to 18 minutes. Reserve ¼ cup of the cooking liquid; drain the potatoes and return to the pot. Mash with 3 Tbsp oil, ¼ tsp each salt and pepper and 2 Tbsp of the reserved cooking liquid (add more liquid if necessary).

❷ While the potatoes are cooking, heat the remaining Tbsp oil in a large skillet over medium heat. Add the onion and ¼ tsp each salt and pepper and cook, covered, stirring occasionally, until tender, 8 to 10 minutes.

❸ Heat broiler. Add the beef to the onion and cook, breaking it up with a spoon, until no longer pink, 5 to 6 minutes. Spoon off and discard any grease. Add the tomatoes and cook, stirring occasionally, for 4 minutes. In a bowl, whisk together the ketchup, vinegar, mustard, molasses and Worcestershire; add to the beef and cook, stirring, for 1 minute.

❹ Transfer the beef mixture to a 2-qt broiler-proof baking dish and top with the mashed potatoes. Broil until it begins to brown, 2 to 4 minutes.

PER SERVING 439 cal, 21 g fat (6 g sat fat), 74 mg chol, 639 mg sod, 27 g pro, 36 g car, 3 g fiber

Make ahead » Prepare the casserole, but do not bake. Tightly wrap and refrigerate for up to 2 days. When ready to serve, bake at 375°F until heated through, then broil until golden brown.

Lamb chops with white bean and cucumber salad

ACTIVE 20 MIN • **TOTAL** 20 MIN • **SERVES** 4
COST PER SERVING $3.92

1	tsp plus 2 Tbsp olive oil
8	small lamb loin chops or 4 small shoulder chops
1	tsp chili powder
	Kosher salt and pepper
2	Tbsp fresh lemon juice
1	15-oz can white beans, rinsed
½	seedless cucumber, cut into thin half-moons
2	scallions, thinly sliced
½	cup fresh cilantro or flat-leaf parsley, chopped

1 Heat oven to 400°F. Heat 1 tsp oil in a large skillet over medium-high heat. Season the lamb with the chili powder and ½ tsp each salt and pepper and cook until browned, 2 to 3 minutes per side. Transfer to a rimmed baking sheet and roast to desired doneness, 4 to 6 minutes for medium-rare.

2 Meanwhile, in a large bowl, whisk together the lemon juice, remaining 2 Tbsp oil, ½ tsp salt and ¼ tsp pepper. Add the beans, cucumber and scallions and toss to combine. Fold in the cilantro and serve with the lamb.

PER SERVING 512 cal, 31 g fat (11 g sat fat), 98 mg chol, 1,103 mg sod, 33 g pro, 25 g car, 6 g fiber

Love your leftovers » For a quick Mediterranean-inspired lunch, slice up leftover lamb and stuff it into pita bread. Top with leftover cucumber and bean salad and top with a dollop of yogurt.

SLOW COOKER

French onion beef stew

ACTIVE 10 MIN • **TOTAL** 5 HR 10 MIN OR 8 HR 10 MIN • **SERVES** 4
COST PER SERVING $3.24

8	sprigs fresh thyme, plus 1 tsp leaves
1	14.5-oz can low-sodium chicken broth
1	cup apple juice
4	medium carrots, cut into ¼-in. pieces
2	medium onions, thinly sliced
1½	lb lean beef stew meat, trimmed and cut into ½-in. pieces
	Kosher salt and pepper
3	Tbsp all-purpose flour
4	thick slices country bread
4	oz Gruyère or Swiss cheese, grated (about 1 cup)

1 Tie a piece of thread or kitchen twine around the thyme sprigs and place them in a 5- to 6-qt slow cooker. Add the chicken broth, apple juice, carrots and onions and mix to combine.

2 Season the beef with ½ tsp each salt and pepper; sprinkle with the flour. Add the beef and any excess flour to the slow cooker and mix to combine. Cook, covered, until the beef and vegetables are tender, 7 to 8 hours on low or 4 to 5 hours on high. Spoon off and discard any fat that has risen to the top. Remove and discard the thyme.

3 When the stew has 10 minutes left to cook, heat the broiler. Place the bread on a foil-lined broiler-proof baking sheet. Sprinkle with the cheese and remaining tsp thyme. Broil until the cheese starts to brown, 1 to 2 minutes. Spoon the stew into bowls and top with the Gruyère toasts.

Make ahead » Refrigerate the stew for up to 3 days or freeze for up to 2 months. Thaw in the refrigerator overnight, if frozen. Reheat, in a medium saucepan, covered, gently stirring occasionally. Make the toasts just before serving.

PER SERVING 540 cal, 18 g fat (8 g sat fat), 142 mg chol, 720 mg sod, 53 g pro, 41 g car, 4 g fiber

EASY ENTERTAINING

Red currant-glazed steak with sautéed bok choy

ACTIVE 25 MIN • **TOTAL** 25 MIN • **SERVES** 4

COST PER SERVING $3.69

1	cup long-grain white rice
¼	cup red currant jelly
2	tsp cider vinegar
¼	tsp crushed red pepper flakes (optional)
1½	lb flank steak
	Kosher salt and pepper
1	Tbsp canola oil
4	small heads baby bok choy

❶ Heat broiler. Cook the rice according to package directions. In a small bowl, whisk together the jelly, vinegar and crushed red pepper (if using).

❷ Meanwhile, season the steak with ¼ tsp each salt and pepper and place on a foil-lined broiler-proof baking sheet. Broil to desired doneness, 5 to 8 minutes for medium-rare, basting with the sauce during the last 3 minutes of cooking. Let rest for at least 5 minutes before slicing.

❸ Meanwhile, heat the oil in a large skillet over medium-high heat. Add the bok choy, season with ¼ tsp each salt and pepper and cook, tossing occasionally, until tender, 3 to 4 minutes. Serve with the steak and rice.

♥ **PER SERVING** 472 cal, 12 g fat (4 g sat fat), 56 mg chol, 363 mg sod, 33 g pro, 56 g car, 2 g fiber

---

Switch it up » Bok choy is a mild Chinese vegetable with crunchy light green stalks and tender dark green leaves. If you can't find it in your supermarket, try using Swiss chard or spinach. If using spinach, cook only until just beginning to wilt, about 2 minutes.

Easy beef stroganoff

ACTIVE 25 MIN • **TOTAL** 25 MIN • **SERVES** 4
COST PER SERVING $3.15

- 6 oz egg noodles (half a 12-oz bag)
- 3 Tbsp olive oil
- 1 lb sirloin steak, thinly sliced
   Kosher salt and pepper
- 1 medium onion, thinly sliced
- 1 green bell pepper, thinly sliced
- 1 lb button mushrooms, sliced
- ½ cup dry white wine (optional)
- ½ cup low-sodium chicken broth
- ½ cup lowfat sour cream
- 1 Tbsp Dijon mustard
- ½ tsp Worcestershire sauce
   Chopped parsley, for serving

❶ Cook the egg noodles according to package directions.

❷ Meanwhile, heat 1 Tbsp of the oil in a large skillet over medium-high heat. Season the steak with ¼ tsp each salt and pepper, and cook in 2 batches until browned, 1 minute per side; transfer to a plate.

❸ Reduce heat to medium. Add the onion, bell pepper and 1 Tbsp oil and cook, stirring occasionally, for 5 minutes. Add the mushrooms, the remaining Tbsp oil and ¼ tsp each salt and pepper. Increase heat to medium-high and cook, tossing, until the vegetables are tender, 4 to 5 minutes more.

❹ Add the wine, if using, and simmer for 1 minute. Return the beef to the skillet. Add the broth and simmer until slightly reduced, 2 to 3 minutes. Remove from heat; stir in the sour cream, mustard and Worcestershire. Spoon over the noodles and sprinkle with parsley, if desired.

Prep tip » Freeze the steak for 20 minutes before cutting—the chilled meat will be easier to slice into extra-thin strips.

PER SERVING 554 cal, 29 g fat (9 g sat fat), 89 mg chol, 448 mg sod, 34 g pro, 40 g car, 4 g fiber

FAMILY FAVORITE

Skirt steak with Southwestern creamed corn

ACTIVE 25 MIN • **TOTAL** 25 MIN • **SERVES** 4

COST PER SERVING $3.67

1½	lb skirt steak, cut crosswise into 4 pieces
	Kosher salt and pepper
1	Tbsp olive oil
1	large onion, chopped
4	cups fresh corn kernels (from 4 to 6 ears)
¾	cup lowfat sour cream
¼	cup pickled jalapeño slices, chopped
½	cup fresh cilantro, chopped

❶ Heat the broiler. Line a broiler-proof rimmed baking sheet with foil. Season the steak with ½ tsp each salt and pepper and place on the prepared sheet. Broil to desired doneness, 2 to 4 minutes per side for medium-rare. Let rest for at least 5 minutes before slicing.

❷ Meanwhile, heat the oil in a large skillet over medium heat. Add the onion, ½ tsp salt and ¼ tsp pepper, and cook, stirring occasionally, until tender, 6 to 8 minutes.

❸ Add the corn and cook, stirring often, until just tender, about 3 minutes. Remove from heat and stir in the sour cream. Fold in the jalapeños and cilantro.

PER SERVING 507 cal, 24 g fat (8 g sat fat), 84 mg chol, 727 mg sod, 40 g pro, 36 g car, 4 g fiber

Switch it up » Turn this dish into tacos by stuffing the steak and corn mixture into tortillas and topping with salsa and guacamole.

SLOW COOKER

Chili dogs

ACTIVE 15 MIN • **TOTAL** 4 HR 15 MIN OR 7 HR 15 MIN • **SERVES** 4

COST PER SERVING $1.80

1	28-oz can whole tomatoes
1	Tbsp chili powder
2	tsp ground cumin
1	medium red onion, finely chopped
	Black pepper
8	oz ground beef chuck
4	hot dogs
4	hot dog buns
2	oz sharp Cheddar, shredded
4	pickles, ketchup and mustard, for serving

❶ Place the tomatoes (and their juices) in a 5- to 6-qt slow cooker, breaking them up with your hands as you add them. Stir in the chili powder, cumin, all but 3 Tbsp of the onion and ½ tsp pepper; refrigerate the remaining red onion.

❷ Add the beef, break it up and stir to combine. Cook, covered, until the meat is cooked through and liquid begins to evaporate, 5 to 7 hours on low or 3 to 4 hours on high.

❸ Fifteen minutes before serving, add the hot dogs to the slow cooker and cook, covered, until heated through. Divide the hot dogs among the buns and top with the chili, Cheddar and remaining onion. Serve with pickles, if desired.

PER SERVING 523 cal, 29 g fat (13 g sat fat), 85 mg chol, 1,751 mg sod, 27 g pro, 38 g car, 4 g fiber

Use up the hot dog buns » Make grilled garlic bread: Split leftover hot dog buns in half and gently press on each half to flatten. Brush with olive oil and sprinkle with salt and pepper. Grill until lightly charred, 1 to 2 minutes. Immediately rub with a clove of garlic. Sprinkle with grated Parmesan, if desired.

Steak with potatoes, tomatoes and herb butter

ACTIVE 25 MIN • **TOTAL** 30 MIN • **SERVES** 4
COST PER SERVING $2.96

1	lb small new potatoes, halved
	Kosher salt and pepper
6	Tbsp unsalted butter, at room temperature
1	clove garlic, finely chopped
¼	cup fresh flat-leaf parsley, finely chopped
¼	cup finely chopped fresh chives (optional)
2	Tbsp olive oil
1	1½-lb sirloin steak or London broil (1 in. thick)
4	plum tomatoes, quartered lengthwise

❶ Place the potatoes in a medium saucepan. Cover with cold water and bring to a boil. Add 1 tsp salt, reduce heat and simmer until tender, 15 to 18 minutes. Drain and return to the pot. Meanwhile, in a small bowl, combine the butter, garlic, parsley, chives (if using) and ¼ tsp each salt and pepper; set aside.

❷ Heat 1 Tbsp oil in a large skillet over medium-high heat. Season the steak with ¼ tsp each salt and pepper and cook to desired doneness, 4 to 5 minutes per side for medium-rare. Let rest for at least 5 minutes before slicing.

❸ Add the tomatoes to the skillet, drizzle with the remaining Tbsp oil and season with ¼ tsp each salt and pepper. Cook, tossing, just until tender, about 2 minutes; transfer to plates. Add the herb butter to the potatoes and toss to coat. Serve with the tomatoes and steak.

PER SERVING 662 cal, 46 g fat (21 g sat fat), 173 mg chol, 525 mg sod, 38 g pro, 23 g car, 2 g fiber

FREEZABLE

Picadillo meatballs

ACTIVE 20 MIN • **TOTAL** 25 MIN • **SERVES** 4
COST PER SERVING $1.69

1	cup long-grain white rice
1	Tbsp olive oil
1	medium onion, finely chopped
2	cloves garlic, finely chopped
1¼	lb ground beef
¼	cup pimiento-stuffed olives, sliced
¼	cup raisins, chopped
1	tsp ground cumin
	Kosher salt and pepper
1	14-oz can tomato sauce
½	tsp ground cinnamon
1	Tbsp red wine vinegar
	Chopped fresh cilantro, for serving

Make ahead » Freeze the cooked meatballs and sauce for up to 2 months. Thaw in the refrigerator overnight, then reheat in a medium saucepan, covered, gently stirring occasionally, being careful not to break the meatballs. Cook the rice just before serving.

❶ Cook the rice according to package directions.

❷ Meanwhile, heat the oil over medium-high heat. Add the onion and cook, stirring often, until tender, 3 to 4 minutes. Stir in the garlic and cook for 1 minute; remove from heat.

❸ Heat broiler. Transfer half the onion mixture to a large bowl. Add the beef, olives, raisins, cumin and ¼ tsp each salt and pepper and mix to combine. Form the mixture into 1½-in. balls (about 20) and place on a foil-lined broiler-proof baking sheet. Broil until cooked through, 6 to 8 minutes.

❹ While the meatballs cook, return the skillet with the remaining onion mixture to medium heat. Add the tomato sauce and cinnamon and simmer until heated through, about 3 minutes; stir in the vinegar. Add the meatballs to the sauce and toss to coat. Serve over the rice and sprinkle with the cilantro, if desired.

PER SERVING 540 cal, 20 g fat (6 g sat fat), 87 mg chol, 871 mg sod, 31 g pro, 58 g car, 3 g fiber

EASY ENTERTAINING

Arugula, steak and crispy potato salad with lemony vinaigrette

ACTIVE 30 MIN • **TOTAL** 30 MIN • **SERVES** 4
COST PER SERVING $4.02

3	shallots
6	Tbsp olive oil
1	lb medium Yukon gold potatoes, sliced ¼ in. thick
1½	lb skirt steak, cut crosswise into 6 pieces
	Kosher salt and pepper
1	lemon
½	cup fresh flat-leaf parsley, finely chopped
2	tsp capers, chopped
1	clove garlic, finely chopped
1	bunch arugula, thick stems discarded

1 Heat the broiler. Line a broiler-proof rimmed baking sheet with foil. Thinly slice 2 shallots. Heat 2 Tbsp oil in a large skillet over medium heat. Add the potatoes and cook, turning occasionally, for 5 minutes. Add the sliced shallots and cook, turning the potatoes occasionally, until they are golden brown and tender, 5 to 6 minutes more. Transfer the vegetables to a plate and cover with foil to keep warm.

2 Season the steak with ½ tsp each salt and pepper and transfer to the prepared sheet. Broil to desired doneness, 2 to 4 minutes per side for medium-rare. Transfer to a cutting board and let rest for at least 5 minutes before slicing.

3 While the steak cooks, make the dressing: Finely chop the remaining shallot and place in a medium bowl. Finely grate 2 tsp lemon zest into the bowl, then squeeze in 2 Tbsp of juice.

4 Stir in the parsley, capers, garlic and ¼ tsp each salt and pepper. Gradually whisk in the remaining 4 Tbsp oil. Arrange the arugula, steak and vegetables on a platter. Drizzle with the dressing.

PER SERVING 574 cal, 36 g fat (9 g sat fat), 77 mg chol, 516 mg sod, 37 g pro, 25 g car, 2 g fiber

Cook's tip » This dressing also makes a tasty marinade. Marinate boneless, skinless chicken breasts or salmon for 20 minutes and pork tenderloin or chops for 45 minutes before broiling or grilling.

SLOW COOKER

Beef soft tacos with pineapple salsa

ACTIVE 10 MIN • **TOTAL** 5 HR 10 MIN OR 8 HR 10 MIN • **SERVES** 4

COST PER SERVING $3.85

1	large red onion
1½	lb flank steak, cut crosswise into 4 pieces
1	Tbsp chili powder
1	tsp ancho chile powder (optional)
½	pineapple (about 2 lb), peeled, cored, and cut into ½-in. pieces
	Kosher salt and pepper
1	jalapeño (seeded for less heat, if desired), thinly sliced
2	Tbsp fresh lime juice
1	avocado, diced
½	cup fresh cilantro
8	small flour tortillas, warmed

❶ Chop ¾ of the onion and refrigerate the rest until ready to use. In a 5- to 6-qt slow cooker, toss the chopped onion, beef, chili powder, ancho chile powder (if using), half the pineapple, ½ tsp salt and ¼ tsp pepper.

❷ Cook, covered, until the meat is tender and shreds easily, 7 to 8 hours on low or 4 to 5 hours on high.

❸ 25 minutes before serving, thinly slice the remaining onion. In a medium bowl, toss the onion, jalapeño, lime juice, remaining pineapple and ¼ tsp each salt and pepper. Fold in the avocado and cilantro.

❹ Using two forks, shred the meat, then stir it into the cooking liquid. Fill the tortillas with the beef mixture and top with the pineapple salsa.

PER SERVING 604 cal, 23 g fat (8 g sat fat), 111 mg chol, 1,073 mg sod, 44 g pro, 56 g car, 8 g fiber

Switch it up » Try this dish with pork instead of beef. Replace the flank steak with 1½ lb pork shoulder (trimmed of excess fat and cut into 3-in. pieces) and cook as directed.

p73

p74

p76

Pork

p77

p78

p80

EASY ENTERTAINING

Spiced pork chops with pineapple-cilantro rice

ACTIVE 25 MIN • **TOTAL** 25 MIN • **SERVES** 4

COST PER SERVING $1.74

- 1 cup long-grain white rice
- 1 Tbsp paprika
- 2 tsp ground cumin
- ¼ tsp ground cinnamon
  Kosher salt and pepper
- 1 Tbsp olive oil
- 4 bone-in pork chops (about 1 in. thick)
- 1 medium red onion, sliced
- 1 8-oz can crushed pineapple, drained
- ½ cup fresh cilantro, roughly chopped

❶ Heat oven to 425°F. Cook the rice according to package directions.

❷ Meanwhile, in a small bowl, combine the paprika, cumin, cinnamon, ¾ tsp salt and ½ tsp pepper. Heat the oil in a large oven-safe skillet over medium-high heat. Season the pork with the spice mixture and cook until golden brown, 2 minutes per side. Scatter the onion around the pork and roast until the pork is just cooked through, 4 to 5 minutes.

❸ Fluff the rice with a fork and toss with the pineapple and roasted onion. Fold in the cilantro and serve with the pork chops.

PER SERVING 510 cal, 18 g fat (5 g sat fat), 101 mg chol, 450 mg sod, 35 g pro, 50 g car, 3 g fiber

Love your leftovers » For dinner, thinly slice leftover pork and stir-fry until heated through. Add the leftover rice mixture and cook, tossing occasionally, until the edges begin to crisp. Toss with 1 Tbsp each soy sauce and rice vinegar, transfer to plates and serve topped with a sunny-side-up egg.

Pork and black bean soup

ACTIVE 15 MIN • **TOTAL** 6 HR 15 MIN OR 8 HR 15 MIN • **SERVES** 6

COST PER SERVING $1.24

6	cups low-sodium chicken broth
1	large red onion, chopped
4	cloves garlic, finely chopped
1	Tbsp chopped canned chipotle chiles in adobo sauce, plus 2 Tbsp sauce
2	tsp ground cumin
1	lb dried black beans, rinsed
1½	lb boneless pork shoulder, trimmed of excess fat
	Kosher salt
	Sour cream, refrigerated fresh salsa and cilantro, for serving

❶ In a 6-qt slow cooker, combine the chicken broth, onion, garlic, chiles, adobo sauce and cumin.

❷ Add the beans and pork; cook, covered, until beans are tender and pork easily pulls apart, 8 hours on low or 6 hours on high.

❸ Transfer pork to a bowl and, using a fork, break into large pieces. Using a handheld immersion blender, purée half the soup. (Alternatively, purée half the soup in a standard blender, then return to the slow cooker.)

❹ Stir the pork back into the soup and season with 1 tsp salt. Serve with the sour cream, salsa and cilantro, if desired.

PER SERVING 526 cal, 18 g fat (7 g sat fat), 91 mg chol, 629 mg sod, 42 g pro, 49 g car, 17 g fiber

Make ahead » Freeze the soup for up to 3 months. Thaw in the refrigerator overnight, then reheat in a medium saucepan, covered, stirring occasionally.

Spanish-style tortilla with salami and potatoes

ACTIVE 20 MIN • **TOTAL** 35 MIN • **SERVES** 4
COST PER SERVING $1.96

¼	lb thinly sliced salami, halved
1	large onion, chopped
¾	lb medium red potatoes (about 2), cut in ½-in. pieces
3	Tbsp olive oil
	Kosher salt and pepper
¼	cup fresh flat-leaf parsley, roughly chopped, plus 1 cup leaves
8	large eggs
4	oz sharp white Cheddar, grated (about 1 cup)
1	Tbsp red wine vinegar
2	tsp Dijon mustard
1	cup grape tomatoes, halved

❶ Heat oven to 400°F. Cook the salami in a large oven-safe nonstick skillet over medium heat until it begins to brown, about 1 minute per side; transfer to a plate.

❷ Add the onion, potatoes, 1 Tbsp oil, ½ tsp salt and ¼ tsp pepper to the skillet and cook, stirring occasionally, until the potatoes are golden brown and just tender, 10 to 12 minutes; stir in the chopped parsley and salami.

❸ Whisk together the eggs and cheese, pour into the skillet and stir to distribute the ingredients. Transfer the skillet to the oven and bake until the tortilla is

Love your leftovers » This egg dish makes a hearty appetizer. Cut any leftovers into squares and serve warm or at room temperature.

puffed, brown around the edges and a knife inserted in the center comes out clean, 10 to 12 minutes.

❹ Meanwhile, in a medium bowl, whisk together the vinegar, mustard, remaining 2 Tbsp oil, and ¼ tsp each salt and pepper. Add the tomatoes and toss to coat; fold in the parsley leaves. Serve with the tortilla.

PER SERVING 551 cal, 38 g fat (14 g sat fat), 431 mg chol, 1,358 mg sod, 30 g pro, 24 g car, 4 g fiber

UNDER 400 CALORIES

Sweet and sour pork and vegetable stir-fry

ACTIVE 30 MIN • **TOTAL** 30 MIN • **SERVES** 4
COST PER SERVING $1.54

1   cup long-grain white rice
2   Tbsp hoisin sauce
1   Tbsp fresh lime juice
2   Tbsp canola oil
2   carrots, cut into matchsticks
1   red pepper, cut into thin strips
½   lb pork tenderloin, thinly sliced
     Kosher salt and pepper
1   cup bean sprouts (optional)
2   scallions, thinly sliced on a diagonal

Use up the hoisin sauce » Hoisin sauce is a sweet and tangy Chinese sauce often used in barbecue or stir-fry recipes or for dipping. Combine hoisin with ketchup for an easy Asian-style glaze.

❶ Cook the rice according to package directions. In a small bowl, whisk together the hoisin, lime juice and 1 Tbsp water; set aside.

❷ Heat 1 Tbsp oil in a large skillet over medium heat. Add the carrots and red pepper and cook, tossing frequently, until the vegetables are just tender, 4 to 5 minutes. Transfer to a bowl.

❸ Return the skillet to the stove and heat the remaining Tbsp oil over medium-high heat. Season the pork with ¼ tsp each salt and pepper and cook, tossing occasionally, until browned, 3 to 4 minutes. Add the hoisin mixture and cook for 1 minute.

❹ Return the vegetables to the skillet, add the bean sprouts (if using) and cook, tossing, until heated through, about 2 minutes. Serve over the rice and sprinkle with the scallions.

♥ **PER SERVING** 360 cal, 9 g fat (1 g sat fat), 37 mg chol, 306 mg sod, 18 g pro, 51 g car, 3 g fiber

20-MINUTE MEAL

Grilled pork chops and sweet potato wedges

ACTIVE 20 MIN • **TOTAL** 20 MIN • **SERVES** 4

COST PER SERVING $3.00

4   small sweet potatoes
    (about 1½ lb total),
    cut into ½-in.-thick wedges

1   Tbsp olive oil
    Kosher salt and pepper

2   scallions, chopped

4   1-in.-thick bone-in pork chops
    (about 2 lb total)

2   tsp ground cumin

4   Tbsp Dijon mustard

1 Heat grill to medium-high. In a large bowl, toss the sweet potatoes with the oil and ¼ tsp each salt and pepper. Place the sweet potato wedges on the grill (set the bowl aside, but do not clean) and cook, turning often, until tender and slightly charred, 12 to 14 minutes. Transfer the potatoes back to the bowl and toss with the scallions.

2 While the potatoes are grilling, season the pork chops with the cumin and ¼ tsp each salt and pepper. Spread both sides of each pork chop with the mustard and grill until cooked through, 5 to 7 minutes per side. Serve with the potatoes.

PER SERVING 457 cal, 21 g fat (5 g sat fat), 107 mg chol, 743 mg sod, 35 g pro, 29 g car, 5 g fiber

Cook's tip » Make this dish for 8 by doubling the potatoes and using 3 small pork tenderloins (about 3½ lb total), which take up less room on the grill, instead of chops. Season as directed and grill, turning occasionally, until a thermometer registers 145°F, 18 to 22 minutes; let rest for 5 minutes before slicing.

Sausage, pepper and cornbread skillet pie

ACTIVE 20 MIN • **TOTAL** 40 MIN • **SERVES** 6
COST PER SERVING $1.66

- 2 tsp olive oil
- 1 lb Italian sausage links
- 2 large red bell peppers, sliced
- 1 large onion, sliced
- 3 cloves garlic, finely chopped
- 1 bunch Swiss chard, stems discarded, leaves coarsely chopped (about 8 cups)
  Kosher salt and pepper
- 1 8.5-oz box corn muffin mix
- ½ cup grated Parmesan (2 oz)
- ⅓ cup milk
- 1 large egg

1 Heat oven to 400°F. Heat the oil in a large cast-iron skillet over medium heat. Add the sausage and cook, turning, until browned on all sides, 3 to 4 minutes. Transfer the sausages to a cutting board and cut into 1-in. pieces.

2 Add the peppers and onion to the skillet and cook, stirring occasionally, for 4 minutes; stir in the garlic. Add the chard, ½ tsp salt and ¼ tsp pepper, and cook until the chard begins to wilt, 1 to 2 minutes. Remove from heat and stir in the sausage.

3 Meanwhile, in a bowl, whisk together the corn muffin mix, Parmesan and ¼ tsp pepper. Add the milk and egg and mix to combine. Spread the batter over the sausage mixture, leaving a ½-in. border all the way around the pan. Bake until golden brown and a toothpick inserted into the cornbread comes out clean, 15 to 20 minutes.

PER SERVING 456 cal, 25 g fat (10 g sat fat), 98 mg chol, 1,255 mg sod, 21 g pro, 37 g car, 3 g fiber

Flavor boost » Vary the flavor by mixing up the sausage. Hot Italian sausage gives this dish a spicy kick, while andouille and kielbasa add smokiness.

EASY ENTERTAINING

Roasted almond and herb-crusted pork tenderloin

ACTIVE 20 MIN • **TOTAL** 30 MIN • **SERVES** 4

COST PER SERVING $1.75

- ¼ cup roasted almonds
- 4 cloves garlic
- 1 slice country bread, crust removed and bread torn into 1-in. pieces
- ¼ cup fresh flat-leaf parsley, roughly chopped
- 1 1¼-lb pork tenderloin
  Kosher salt and pepper
- 1 Tbsp Dijon mustard
- 2 Tbsp olive oil
- 1 bunch spinach, thick stems discarded

Love your leftovers » For a delicious next-day lunch, layer the leftover sliced pork and spinach on toasted bread and top with some sliced provolone.

① Heat oven to 400°F. Line a rimmed baking sheet with parchment paper or foil. In a food processor, roughly chop the almonds and 2 cloves garlic. Add the bread and parsley and pulse until small crumbs form.

② Season the pork with ¼ tsp each salt and pepper, then spread with the mustard. Coat with the bread crumb mixture, pressing gently to help it adhere. Transfer the pork to the prepared baking sheet and roast until the internal temperature reaches 145°F, 18 to 22 minutes. Let rest for at least 5 minutes before slicing.

③ Meanwhile, thinly slice the remaining 2 cloves garlic. Heat the oil in a large skillet over medium heat. Add the garlic and cook, stirring, until golden brown, about 2 minutes. Add the spinach and ¼ tsp each salt and pepper and cook, tossing, until spinach begins to wilt, about 2 minutes. Serve with the pork.

♥ **PER SERVING** 316 cal, 16 g fat (3 g sat fat), 83 mg chol, 492 mg sod, 34 g pro, 10 g car, 3 g fiber

SLOW COOKER

Smoky split pea soup

ACTIVE 15 MIN • **TOTAL** 5 HR 15 MIN OR 8 HR 15 MIN • **SERVES** 6
COST PER SERVING $1.38

1	lb green split peas, rinsed
4	medium carrots, cut into ½-in. pieces
2	medium parsnips, cut into ½-in. pieces
2	stalks celery, cut into ½-in. pieces
2	cloves garlic, finely chopped
1	large onion, chopped
½	tsp dried thyme
2	ham hocks (about 1½ lb total)
	Kosher salt and pepper

❶ In a 5- to 6-qt slow cooker, combine the split peas, carrots, parsnips, celery, garlic, onion, thyme and 6 cups water. Add the ham hocks.

❷ Cook, covered, until the meat is tender and easily pulls apart, 7 to 8 hours on low or for 4 to 5 hours on high.

❸ Transfer the ham hocks to a plate. When cool enough to handle, shred the meat, discarding the skin and bones. Stir back into the soup along with ½ tsp salt and ¼ tsp pepper.

♥ **PER SERVING** 394 cal, 2 g fat (2 g sat fat), 19 mg chol, 259 mg sod, 23 g pro, 65 g car, 31 g fiber

Make ahead » Freeze the soup for up to 3 months. Thaw in the refrigerator overnight, then reheat in a medium saucepan, covered, stirring occasionally.

Pork chops with balsamic braised cabbage

ACTIVE 25 MIN • **TOTAL** 25 MIN • **SERVES** 4
COST PER SERVING $2.73

- **3** Tbsp olive oil
- **4** bone-in pork chops (about 1 in. thick)
  Kosher salt and pepper
- **1** large onion, sliced
- **½** small head red cabbage (about 1 lb), cored and thinly sliced
- **¼** cup balsamic vinegar
- **½** cup fresh flat-leaf parsley, chopped
  Mashed potatoes, for serving

1 Heat oven to 400°F. Heat 1 Tbsp oil in a large skillet over medium-high heat. Season the pork with ½ tsp salt and ¼ tsp pepper, and cook until browned, 2 to 3 minutes per side. Transfer to a rimmed baking sheet and roast until just cooked through, 5 to 6 minutes.

2 Meanwhile, wipe out the skillet and heat the remaining 2 Tbsp oil over medium heat. Add the onion and cook, covered, stirring occasionally, for 5 minutes.

3 Add the cabbage, vinegar, 2 Tbsp water, ½ tsp salt and ¼ tsp pepper and cook, covered, stirring occasionally, until the cabbage is just tender, 5 to 6 minutes. Fold in the parsley and serve with the pork chops and potatoes, if desired.

PER SERVING 589 cal, 34 g fat (8 g sat fat), 91 mg chol, 603 mg sod, 35 g pro, 34 g car, 4 g fiber

SLOW COOKER

Orange stewed pork with okra

ACTIVE 25 MIN • **TOTAL** 6 HR 25 MIN OR 8HR 25 MIN • **SERVES** 4
COST PER SERVING $1.83

1	large navel orange
1	Tbsp all-purpose flour
1	Tbsp paprika
1	Tbsp ground cumin
½	tsp ground cinnamon
	Kosher salt and pepper
1	14.5-oz can diced tomatoes
4	cloves garlic, smashed
2	lb boneless pork shoulder, trimmed well and cut into 1½-in. pieces
8	oz frozen cut okra
	Polenta, for serving

Top it off » Make quick pickled onions by tossing 1 small red onion (thinly sliced) with 2 Tbsp fresh lime juice and ¼ tsp each salt and pepper. Let sit, tossing occasionally, until slightly softened, about 12 minutes.

1 Zest the orange into a 5- to 6-qt slow cooker. Squeeze the juice of the orange into the slow cooker (you should have about ¾ cup). Whisk in the flour, paprika, cumin, cinnamon and ½ tsp each salt and pepper.

2 Add the tomatoes (and their juices), garlic and pork and toss to combine. Cook, covered, until the pork is tender and easily pulls apart, on low for 7 to 8 hours or on high for 5 to 6 hours.

3 Gently fold the okra into the stew, cover and cook for 6 minutes. Serve with polenta, if desired.

PER SERVING 390 cal, 14 g fat (5 g sat fat), 136 mg chol, 637 mg sod, 45 g pro, 18 g car, 4 g fiber

UNDER 400 CALORIES

Spiced pork with black-eyed pea salad

ACTIVE 10 MIN • **TOTAL** 30 MIN • **SERVES** 4

COST PER SERVING $1.92

4	tsp olive oil
1	1¼-lb pork tenderloin
1	tsp chili powder
1	tsp ground cumin
	Kosher salt and pepper
1	15-oz can black-eyed peas, rinsed
½	seedless cucumber, cut into ¼-in. pieces
3	scallions, chopped
1	jalapeño (seeded for less heat, if desired), finely chopped
½	cup fresh cilantro, chopped
2	Tbsp fresh lime juice

① Heat oven to 400°F. Heat 2 tsp of the oil in a large ovenproof skillet over medium-high heat. Season the pork with the chili powder, cumin and ¼ tsp each salt and pepper and cook, turning, until browned on all sides, 6 to 8 minutes total.

② Transfer the skillet to the oven and roast until the pork reach 145°F, 12 to 14 minutes. Transfer the pork to a cutting board and let rest at least 5 minutes before slicing.

③ Meanwhile, in a large bowl, combine the peas, cucumber, scallions, jalapeño, cilantro, lime juice, remaining 2 tsp oil, and ¼ tsp each salt and pepper. Serve with the pork.

♥ **PER SERVING** 243 cal, 7 g fat (2 g sat fat), 72 mg chol, 535 mg sod, 32 g pro, 16 g car, 5 g fiber

Switch it up » Serve this black-eyed pea salad as a tasty side with chicken, fish or beef. Or for a vegetarian main, toss with 1 bunch fresh spinach (thick stems discarded).

Pulled pork sandwiches with cabbage slaw

ACTIVE 15 MIN • **TOTAL** 5 HR 15 MIN OR 8 HR 15 MIN • **SERVES** 4
COST PER SERVING $1.58

½   cup ketchup

¼   cup packed brown sugar

1   Tbsp chili powder

¼   cup plus 2 Tbsp cider vinegar
    Kosher salt and pepper

1   1½-lb pork butt or shoulder, trimmed
    and cut into 3-in. pieces

½   cup lowfat sour cream

½   small green cabbage (about 1 lb)

½   cup fresh cilantro

4   rolls, split
    Potato chips and pickles, for serving

Switch it up » Try this dish with beef or chicken instead of pork. Replace the pork with a 2-lb brisket (trimmed of excess fat) and cook as directed. Or use 2 lb boneless, skinless chicken thighs and decrease the cooking times by 2 hours.

❶ In a 5- to 6-qt slow cooker, whisk together the ketchup, sugar, chili powder, ¼ cup vinegar and ½ tsp each salt and pepper.

❷ Add the pork and toss to coat. Cook, covered, until the pork is tender and shreds easily, 7 to 8 hours on low or 4 to 5 hours on high.

❸ Forty-five minutes before serving, in a large bowl, whisk together the sour cream, remaining 2 Tbsp vinegar, 1 Tbsp water and ½ tsp each salt and pepper. Core and thinly slice the cabbage, add it to the sour cream mixture and toss to coat. Let sit, tossing occasionally. Fold in the cilantro before serving.

❹ Using two forks, shred the pork into large pieces; gently toss in the cooking liquid. Fill the rolls with the pork and slaw. Serve with chips and pickles, if desired.

PER SERVING 565 cal, 22 g fat (8 g sat fat), 115 mg chol, 1,228 mg sod, 40 g pro, 53 g car, 4 g fiber

5-INGREDIENT MEAL*

Roasted sausage, apples, leeks and potatoes

ACTIVE 5 MIN • **TOTAL** 35 MIN • **SERVES** 4
COST PER SERVING $2.29

- 2   small crisp red apples (such as Empire or Braeburn), quartered
- 2   leeks (white and light green parts only), halved crosswise and lengthwise
- 2   yellow potatoes (about ½ lb total), cut into ½-in.-thick wedges
- 8   sprigs fresh thyme
- 2   Tbsp olive oil
      Kosher salt and pepper
- 8   small Italian sausage links (about 1½ lb total)
      Whole-grain mustard, for serving

* We consider olive oil, salt and pepper to be staples, so they are not included in the ingredient count for this recipe.

Switch it up » Try substituting Bartlett pears for the apples in this recipe. Like apples, the pears will add a caramelized sweetness to this savory dish.

❶ Heat oven to 425°F. In a large roasting pan, toss the apples, leeks, potatoes, thyme, oil, ½ tsp salt and ¼ tsp pepper. Roast for 15 minutes.

❷ Stir the vegetables and add the sausages to the pan, nestling them among the vegetables. Roast until the sausage is cooked through and the vegetables are tender, 15 to 20 minutes more.

PER SERVING 418 cal, 19 g fat (4 g sat fat), 83 mg chol, 1,049 mg sod, 26 g pro, 30 g car, 3 g fiber

SLOW COOKER

Asian braised pork

ACTIVE 15 MIN • **TOTAL** 6 HR 15 MIN OR 8 HR 15 MIN • **SERVES** 4

COST PER SERVING $2.28

¼	cup low-sodium soy sauce
½	tsp ground allspice
¼	to ½ tsp crushed red pepper flakes
¼	cup plus 1 Tbsp brown sugar
1	2-in. piece fresh ginger, half thinly sliced and half grated
2½	lb boneless pork shoulder, trimmed and cut into 2-in. pieces
1	cup long-grain white rice
¼	cup rice vinegar
	Kosher salt and pepper
1	seedless cucumber, thinly sliced into half-moons
¼	sweet onion, thinly sliced

❶ In a 5- to 6-qt slow cooker, combine the soy sauce, allspice, crushed red pepper, ¼ cup of the brown sugar and the sliced ginger. Add the pork and toss to coat. Cover and cook until the meat is tender, 7 to 8 hours on low or 5 to 6 hours on high.

❷ Thirty minutes before serving, cook the rice according to package directions. In a large bowl, whisk together the vinegar, remaining Tbsp brown sugar, grated ginger, and ¼ tsp each salt and pepper. Add the cucumber and onion and toss to combine.

❸ Spoon the pork over the rice and serve with the cucumber salad.

PER SERVING 641 cal, 16 g fat (6 g sat fat), 166 mg chol, 822 mg sod, 56 g pro, 64 g car, 2 g fiber

Flavor boost » Add extra Asian flair by substituting the allspice with Chinese five-spice powder, typically a blend of star anise, cinnamon, cloves, Szechuan peppercorns and fennel seeds. You'll find it in the spice aisle of most supermarkets.

EASY ENTERTAINING

Sausage, cabbage and red onion galette

ACTIVE 15 MIN • **TOTAL** 40 MIN • **SERVES** 6
COST PER SERVING 96¢

1   red onion, thinly sliced

½   small head cabbage, cored and sliced ½-in. thick (about 4 cups)

2   Tbsp small sprigs fresh thyme

2   Tbsp olive oil

    Kosher salt and pepper

8   oz Italian sausage, casings removed, crumbled into small pieces

3   oz extra-sharp Cheddar, grated

1   refrigerated rolled pie crust

1   large egg, beaten

❶ Heat oven to 400°F. In a large bowl, toss together the onion, cabbage, thyme, oil and ¼ tsp each salt and pepper. Add the sausage and Cheddar and toss to combine.

❷ Working on a piece of parchment paper, roll the pie crust into a 14-in. circle. Slide the paper (and crust) onto a baking sheet. Spoon the cabbage mixture onto the pie crust, leaving a 2½-in. border all the way around. Fold the border of the crust over the cabbage mixture.

❸ Brush the crust with the egg and bake until the crust is golden brown and the vegetables are tender, 20 to 25 minutes. (Cover with foil if the crust is getting dark.)

PER SERVING 413 cal, 32 g fat (12 g sat fat), 79 mg chol, 658 mg sod, 12 g pro, 22 g car, 2 g fiber

Make ahead » Refrigerate the cooked galette for up to 2 days. When ready to serve, bake at 375°F until heated through.

p84

p86

p88

p89

p90

p92

p93

p94

p96

p97

p99

p100

Seafood

p102

p103

p104

ONE-POT

Garlicky roasted shrimp, red peppers and feta

ACTIVE 5 MIN • **TOTAL** 20 MIN • **SERVES** 4
COST PER SERVING $4.19

1½	**lb large peeled and deveined shrimp**
1	**12-oz jar roasted red peppers, drained and cut into 1-in. pieces**
4	**scallions, sliced**
4	**cloves garlic, thinly sliced**
2	**Tbsp dry white wine**
1	**Tbsp fresh lemon juice, plus wedges for serving**
	Kosher salt and pepper
2	**Tbsp olive oil**
4	**oz feta cheese, crumbled**
	Flatbread, for serving

❶ Heat oven to 425°F. In a 1½- to 2-qt baking dish, toss together the shrimp, roasted peppers, scallions, garlic, wine, lemon juice and ¼ tsp each salt and pepper.

❷ Drizzle with the oil and sprinkle with feta. Bake until the shrimp are opaque throughout, 12 to 15 minutes. Serve with the lemon wedges and flatbread, if desired.

PER SERVING 280 cal, 15 g fat (2 g sat fat), 240 mg chol, 1,587 mg sod, 28 g pro, 8 g car, 1 g fiber

Switch it up » For a Mediterranean-inspired pasta, toss the roasted shrimp mixture with 12 oz cooked angel hair and 1 Tbsp fresh lemon juice.

EASY ENTERTAINING

Grilled Cajun salmon, tomatoes and green beans

ACTIVE 25 MIN • **TOTAL** 25 MIN • **SERVES** 4

COST PER SERVING $2.16

½ cup fresh cilantro, roughly chopped

2 scallions, chopped

2 Tbsp fresh lime juice, plus wedges for serving

4 Tbsp olive oil

Kosher salt and pepper

4 plum tomatoes, halved

¾ lb green beans

1¼ lb skinless salmon fillet, cut into 4 pieces

2 tsp Cajun or blackening seasoning (no salt added)

1 Heat grill to medium-high. In a small bowl, combine the cilantro, scallions, lime juice, 3 Tbsp oil and ½ tsp each salt and pepper; set aside.

2 In a bowl, toss the tomatoes, green beans, remaining Tbsp oil and ¼ tsp each salt and pepper. Season the salmon with the Cajun seasoning and ¼ tsp salt.

3 Grill the salmon until opaque throughout, 3 to 4 minutes per side. Grill the beans and tomatoes, turning the beans often and the tomatoes once, until tender and charred, 3 to 5 minutes.

4 Drizzle the salmon and vegetables with the cilantro vinaigrette. Serve with lime wedges, if desired.

♥ **PER SERVING** 337 cal, 19 g fat (3 g sat fat), 66 mg chol, 443 mg sod, 31 g pro, 11 g car, 4 g fiber

Love your leftovers » Make a pasta salad by chopping any leftover tomatoes and green beans and tossing with cooked pasta, baby spinach, olive oil and red wine vinegar.

Shrimp and corn chowder

ACTIVE 15 MIN • **TOTAL** 30 MIN • **SERVES** 4
COST PER SERVING $2.83

4	slices bacon (about 4 oz)
2	Tbsp olive oil
1	medium onion, chopped
	Kosher salt and pepper
½	lb Yukon gold potatoes (peeled, if desired), cut into ½-in. pieces
1	cup dry white wine
2	stalks celery, thinly sliced
1	cup corn kernels (cut from 1 ear or frozen and thawed)
¾	lb medium peeled and deveined shrimp
½	cup heavy cream
¼	cup fresh flat-leaf parsley, chopped
	Crusty bread, for serving

1 Cook the bacon in a large saucepan over medium heat until crisp, 5 to 6 minutes. Transfer to a paper towel–lined plate; break into pieces when cool.

2 Wipe out the saucepan and heat the oil over medium heat. Add the onion, ½ tsp salt and ¼ tsp pepper and cook, stirring occasionally, for 5 minutes.

3 Add the potatoes, wine and 2½ cups water and bring to a boil. Reduce heat and simmer until the potatoes are just tender, 12 to 15 minutes. Stir in the celery, corn, shrimp and cream, and simmer until the shrimp are opaque throughout, 3 to 4 minutes. Top with the bacon and parsley. Serve with the bread, if desired.

Switch it up » Instead of shrimp add 12 seared sea scallops to the chowder before serving: Pat the scallops dry with a paper towel, season with salt and pepper, and cook in oil over medium-high heat until golden brown and opaque throughout, 2 to 3 minutes per side.

PER SERVING: 381 cal, 23 g fat (9 g sat fat), 159 mg chol, 996 mg sod, 19 g pro, 24 g car, 3 g fiber

UNDER 400 CALORIES

Seared tilapia with pineapple and cucumber relish

ACTIVE 15 MIN • **TOTAL** 20 MIN • **SERVES** 4

COST PER SERVING $3.20

1	cup long-grain white rice
2	Tbsp fresh lime juice
1	Tbsp fresh grated ginger
2	tsp honey
2	Tbsp plus 1 tsp olive oil
	Kosher salt and pepper
2	scallions, thinly sliced
1	jalapeño (seeded, if desired), finely chopped
½	small pineapple (about 1 lb), peeled, cored and cut into small pieces
1	small English cucumber, cut into small pieces
4	6-oz tilapia fillets

1 Cook the rice according to package directions.

2 Meanwhile, in a large bowl, whisk together the lime juice, ginger, honey, 2 Tbsp oil and ¼ tsp each salt and pepper. Toss with the scallions, jalapeño, pineapple and cucumber.

3 Heat the remaining tsp oil in a large nonstick skillet over medium heat. Season the tilapia with ¼ tsp each salt and pepper and cook until golden brown and opaque throughout, 1 to 3 minutes per side. Serve the fish with the rice and relish.

♥ **PER SERVING** 382 cal, 9 g fat (1 g sat fat), 77 mg chol, 207 mg sod, 40 g pro, 51 g car, 1 g fiber

Switch it up » Try making the relish with 1 ripe mango instead of the pineapple, or use a combination of both.

NO COOK

Tuna-stuffed tomatoes

ACTIVE 15 MIN • **TOTAL** 15 MIN • **SERVES** 4
COST PER SERVING $1.47

4	large tomatoes
2	5-oz cans solid white tuna, drained
2	stalks celery, halved lengthwise and thinly sliced
2	Tbsp capers, roughly chopped
1	Tbsp olive oil
1	Tbsp red wine vinegar
	Kosher salt and pepper
½	cup fresh flat-leaf parsley
	Crusty bread, for serving

❶ With a sharp knife, slice a very thin piece off the bottom and ¼ in. off the top of each tomato. With a spoon, scoop out the seeds and pulp. Roughly chop the pulp and tomato bottoms and place in a large bowl.

❷ Add the tuna, celery, capers, oil, vinegar and ¼ tsp each salt and pepper, and toss to combine; fold in the parsley.

❸ Spoon the tuna mixture into the tomatoes. Serve with the tops and bread, if desired.

♥ **PER SERVING** 162 cal, 6 g fat (1 g sat fat), 30 mg chol, 558 mg sod, 19 g pro, 9 g car, 3 g fiber

Make ahead » Prepare the tuna mixture without the tomato and parsley and refrigerate for up to 2 days. To serve, cut the tomatoes as directed and fold in the chopped tomatoes and parsley into the tuna mixture. Stuff the tomatoes with the tuna salad.

Switch it up » Serve this bright, zingy salad with sliced steak, lamb or crispy chicken cutlets.

20-MINUTE MEAL

Fish with gingery cucumbers

ACTIVE 20 MIN • **TOTAL** 20 MIN • **SERVES** 4
COST PER SERVING $2.70

2	Tbsp rice vinegar
1	Tbsp fresh grated ginger
2	Tbsp plus 1 tsp olive oil
	Kosher salt and pepper
1	bunch radishes, thinly sliced
1	small seedless cucumber, thinly sliced into half-moons
4	oz snow peas, thinly sliced lengthwise
½	small sweet onion, thinly sliced
4	6-oz pieces skinless white fish fillet (such as cod, striped bass or tilapia)
¼	cup fresh mint, thinly sliced

1 In a large bowl, whisk together the vinegar, ginger, 2 Tbsp oil and ¼ tsp each salt and pepper. Add the radishes, cucumber, snow peas and onion and toss to combine.

2 Heat the remaining tsp oil in a large nonstick skillet over medium heat. Season the fish with ¼ tsp each salt and pepper and cook until golden brown and opaque throughout, 3 to 4 minutes per side. Fold the mint into the cucumber-radish salad and serve with the fish.

♥ **PER SERVING** 224 cal, 9 g fat (1 g sat fat), 65 mg chol, 340 mg sod, 29 g pro, 6 g car, 2 g fiber

EASY ENTERTAINING

Salmon and couscous salad with snap peas and mint

ACTIVE 20 MIN • **TOTAL** 30 MIN • **SERVES** 4
COST PER SERVING $1.80

- 1 Tbsp plus 1 tsp olive oil
- 1 1 lb piece skinless salmon fillet
  Kosher salt and black pepper
- 1 cup whole-wheat couscous
- 1 small orange
- ¼ cup snap peas, sliced crosswise (about 1 cup)
- ½ small red onion, thinly sliced
- 1 cup fresh flat-leaf parsley, roughly chopped
- ¼ cup fresh mint, torn

Make ahead » Prepare the fish and salad without the parsley and mint. Refrigerate the salmon and salad separately for up to 2 days. To serve, let the salad stand at room temperature for 5 minutes. Flake the fish and fold into the couscous and vegetables along with the herbs.

1 Heat 1 tsp oil in a nonstick skillet over medium heat. Season the salmon with ¼ tsp each salt and pepper, and cook until opaque throughout, 4 to 6 minutes per side; transfer to a plate and refrigerate for 15 minutes.

2 Meanwhile, place the couscous in a large bowl. Add 1 cup hot water, cover and let sit for 5 minutes; fluff with a fork.

3 Using a vegetable peeler, remove 3 strips of zest from the orange and thinly slice on a diagonal. Squeeze 2 Tbsp orange juice into the couscous and toss with the zest, snap peas, onion, parsley, mint, remaining Tbsp oil, ½ tsp salt and ¼ tsp pepper.

4 Using a fork, flake the cooled salmon into large pieces and gently fold into the couscous and vegetables.

♥ **PER SERVING** 424 cal, 13 g fat (2 g sat fat), 72 mg chol, 432 mg sod, 34 g pro, 43 g car, 8 g fiber

NO COOK

Creamy shrimp rolls

ACTIVE 15 MIN • **TOTAL** 15 MIN • **SERVES** 4
COST PER SERVING $2.45

3	Tbsp mayonnaise
1	Tbsp whole-grain mustard
¼	cup cornichons, chopped, plus 1 Tbsp brine
	Black pepper
1	lb cooked, peeled and deveined large shrimp, coarsely chopped
2	tsp chopped fresh tarragon
4	hot dog buns
4	pieces romaine or green-leaf lettuce
	Potato chips, for serving

❶ In a large bowl, whisk together the mayonnaise, mustard, brine and ¼ tsp pepper.

❷ Add the shrimp, cornichons and tarragon and toss to combine.

❸ Line the buns with the lettuce and top with the shrimp mixture. Serve with potato chips, if desired.

PER SERVING 305 cal, 12 g fat (2 g sat fat), 147 mg chol, 1,134 mg sod, 20 g pro, 28 g car, 1 g fiber

Use up the cornichons » Slice the remaining cornichons (small, tart French-style pickles) and pile them onto salami or ham sandwiches. You can also enjoy them chopped and folded into egg or tuna salads.

Roasted salmon, tomatoes and cauliflower

ACTIVE 10 MIN • **TOTAL** 40 MIN • **SERVES** 4
COST PER SERVING $3.42

¼ cup golden raisins

2 small red onions, cut into wedges

1 small head cauliflower (about 1½ lb), cored and sliced ¼ in. thick

1 pint grape tomatoes

2 Tbsp olive oil

Kosher salt and pepper

1 1½-lb piece skinless salmon fillet

½ tsp curry powder

❶ Heat oven to 425°F. Place the raisins in a small pot, add enough water to cover and bring to a boil. Remove the pot from the heat and let sit for 15 minutes. Drain and set aside.

❷ Meanwhile, divide the onions, cauliflower and tomatoes between two large rimmed baking sheets. Toss each with 1 Tbsp oil and ¼ tsp each salt and pepper. Roast for 20 minutes.

❸ Season the salmon with the curry, ½ tsp salt and ¼ tsp pepper. Nestle it among the vegetables on one of the baking sheets. Roast both pans until the salmon is opaque throughout and the vegetables are golden brown and tender, 12 to 15 minutes more.

❹ Cut the salmon into pieces and transfer to plates. Toss the vegetables with the raisins and serve with the salmon.

....

♥ **PER SERVING** 376 cal, 14 g fat (3 g sat fat), 90 mg chol, 488 mg sod, 43 g pro, 18 g car, 3 g fiber

Love your leftovers » For a tasty dinner, warm any leftover cauliflower-tomato mixture in a small saucepan over medium heat. Toss with cooked rigatoni, or any short pasta, and fresh spinach.

FAMILY FAVORITE

Crispy fish with oven fries and smashed peas

ACTIVE 30 MIN • **TOTAL** 30 MIN • **SERVES** 4
COST PER SERVING $3.69

4	medium russet potatoes (about 1½ lb), cut into ½-in.-thick wedges
5	Tbsp olive oil
	Kosher salt and pepper
½	cup panko bread crumbs
¼	cup fresh flat-leaf parsley, chopped
4	6-oz pieces cod fillet (about 1 in. thick)
2	Tbsp Dijon mustard
1	12-oz pkg frozen peas
2	Tbsp prepared horseradish

❶ Heat oven to 425°F. On a large rimmed baking sheet, toss the potatoes with 2 Tbsp oil and ½ tsp each salt and pepper. Roast for 12 minutes.

❷ In a bowl, combine the bread crumbs, parsley and 1 Tbsp oil. Season the fish with ¼ tsp each salt and pepper.

❸ Push the potatoes to the edges of the pan and place the fish in the center. Spread the mustard over the fish and top with the bread crumb mixture. Roast until the potatoes are golden brown and tender and the fish is opaque throughout, 10 to 12 minutes more.

❹ While the fish is cooking, bring a small saucepan of water to a boil. Add the peas and boil until heated through, about 2 minutes. Drain and return them to the pan. Add the horseradish, remaining 2 Tbsp oil and ¼ tsp each salt and pepper and gently smash. Serve with the fish and fries.

Use up the horseradish » Make a spread: Combine 2 Tbsp horseradish with ½ cup sour cream and ¼ tsp each salt and pepper and use as a spread for chicken or roast beef sandwiches.

♥ **PER SERVING** 515 cal, 18 g fat (3 g sat fat), 65 mg chol, 798 mg sod, 36 g pro, 51 g car, 7 g fiber

15-MINUTE MEAL

Tilapia with oranges, tomatoes and toasted garlic

ACTIVE 15 MIN • **TOTAL** 15 MIN • **SERVES** 4
COST PER SERVING $2.89

½	cup whole-wheat couscous
1	large orange
3	tsp olive oil
4	small tilapia fillets (about 1½ lb)
	Kosher salt and pepper
2	cloves garlic, thinly sliced
1	½-in. piece fresh ginger, very thinly sliced
1	pint cherry tomatoes, halved
2	scallions, thinly sliced

❶ Prepare the couscous according to package directions. Cut away the peel and white pith of the orange. Working over a bowl, cut the orange into segments, adding them to the bowl along with any juices.

❷ Heat 1 tsp oil in a nonstick skillet over medium heat. Season the tilapia with ½ tsp salt and ¼ tsp pepper and cook until opaque throughout, 1 to 2 minutes per side. Transfer to a plate and cover with foil to keep warm.

❸ Wipe out the skillet and heat the remaining 2 tsp oil over medium heat. Add the garlic and ginger and cook, stirring occasionally, until golden brown, about 1 minute. Add the tomatoes and cook, tossing occasionally, until they begin to break down, about 3 minutes. Add the oranges and any juices and gently toss to heat through. Serve with the tilapia and couscous and sprinkle with the scallions.

♥ **PER SERVING** 323 cal, 7 g fat (2 g sat fat), 77 mg chol, 322 mg sod, 40 g pro, 28 g car, 5 g fiber

Switch it up » Try the orange and tomato mixture with sautéed shrimp, seared chicken or broiled steak.

EASY ENTERTAINING

Orange and ginger halibut in parchment

ACTIVE 15 MIN • **TOTAL** 30 MIN • **SERVES** 4
COST PER SERVING $3.98

- 1 cup long-grain white rice
- 1 1-in. piece fresh ginger, thinly sliced
- ¼ cup orange marmalade
- 1 Tbsp low-sodium soy sauce
- 4 small baby bok choy, trimmed and leaves separated
- 1 red bell pepper, thinly sliced
- 4 6-oz pieces skinless halibut or cod fillet (¾ in. thick)
   Black pepper
- 2 scallions, thinly sliced

❶ Heat oven to 400°F. Cook the rice according to package directions.

❷ Meanwhile, stack the slices of ginger and thinly slice into small sticks. In a small bowl, combine the marmalade, soy sauce and ginger. Tear off four 12-in. squares of parchment paper or aluminum foil and arrange on 2 baking sheets.

❸ Divide the bok choy and bell pepper among the squares, place the fish on top, season with ½ tsp pepper and spoon the marmalade mixture over the fish. Top each fillet with another square of parchment or foil. Fold each edge up and over 3 times. Then fold each corner of the packet under itself to create a seal that will remain intact while packet is in the oven. Bake for 15 minutes.

❹ Transfer each packet to a plate. Gently lift the top piece of parchment. Using a paring knife or scissors, cut an X in the center. Fold back the triangles, gently tearing open the paper, to expose the meal inside (be careful of the steam). Serve with the scallions, for sprinkling, and the rice.

♥ **PER SERVING** 415 cal, 3 g fat (1 g sat fat), 83 mg chol, 299 mg sod, 37 g pro, 59 g car, 3 g fiber

Cook's tip » Wrapping vegetables and proteins like seafood and chicken in parchment before cooking allows the food to steam inside the wrapper, so it stays moist without needing oil.

Shrimp and broccoli stir-fry

ACTIVE 20 MIN • **TOTAL** 30 MIN • **SERVES** 4
COST PER SERVING $3.20

- 1 cup long-grain white rice
- 1 large navel orange
- 2 tsp cornstarch
- ¼ cup barbecue sauce
- 2 Tbsp low-sodium soy sauce
- 1 bunch broccoli (about 1¼ lb), stalks thinly sliced and heads cut into small florets
- 1 Tbsp canola oil
- 1 lb medium peeled and deveined frozen shrimp, thawed and patted dry
- 2 scallions, sliced

❶ Cook the rice according to package directions.

❷ Using a vegetable peeler, remove 4 strips of zest from the orange; thinly slice the zest and set aside. Squeeze the juice from the orange into a small bowl (you should get about ½ cup); stir in the cornstarch. Add the barbecue and soy sauces and stir to combine.

❸ Bring ½ cup water to a simmer in a large skillet. Add the broccoli and cook, covered, until just tender, 2 to 3 minutes. Using a slotted spoon, transfer the broccoli to a bowl.

❹ Wipe out the skillet, then heat the oil over medium-high heat. Add the shrimp and cook, stirring occasionally, until opaque throughout, about 3 minutes. Add the sauce mixture and simmer until thickened, about 1 minute. Return the broccoli to the skillet and toss to combine.

❺ Fluff the rice with a fork and fold in the orange zest and scallions. Serve with the shrimp and broccoli.

Switch it up » Try this dish with beef, pork or chicken instead of shrimp. Thinly slice sirloin steak, pork tenderloin or boneless, skinless chicken breast and cook, tossing occasionally, until golden brown and cooked through, 2 to 4 minutes.

PER SERVING 399 cal, 6 g fat (1 g sat fat), 143 mg chol, 1,094 mg sod, 24 g pro, 63 g car, 5 g fiber

EASY ENTERTAINING

Seared white fish with olive relish and lemon mashed potatoes

ACTIVE 25 MIN • **TOTAL** 25 MIN • **SERVES** 4
COST PER SERVING $3.46

1½	lb medium Yukon gold potatoes, cut into 2-in. pieces
	Kosher salt and pepper
2	tsp fresh lemon zest
5	Tbsp olive oil
1	cup fresh flat-leaf parsley, chopped
½	cup large pitted green olives, chopped
¼	cup unsalted roasted almonds, chopped
2	Tbsp fresh lemon juice
1	small clove garlic, finely chopped
¼	to ½ tsp crushed red pepper flakes (optional)
4	6-oz pieces skinless white fish fillet (such as cod, striped bass or halibut)

Prep tip » Let your food processor do the chopping: Place the garlic in first, pulsing to roughly chop, then add the rest of the relish ingredients.

❶ Place the potatoes in a large pot. Add enough cold water to cover and bring to a boil. Add 1 tsp salt, reduce heat and simmer until just tender, 15 to 18 minutes. Reserve ½ cup of the cooking liquid, drain the potatoes and return them to the pot. Mash with the lemon zest, 2 Tbsp oil, ¼ tsp each salt and pepper, and 2 Tbsp of the reserved cooking liquid (adding more liquid if necessary).

❷ Meanwhile, in a medium bowl, combine the parsley, olives, almonds, lemon juice, garlic, crushed red pepper (if using) and 2 Tbsp oil; set aside.

❸ Heat the remaining Tbsp oil in a large skillet over medium-high heat. Season the fish with ¼ tsp each salt and pepper, and cook until golden brown and opaque throughout, 3 to 4 minutes per side. Serve with the mashed potatoes and relish.

PER SERVING 465 cal, 24 g fat (3 g sat fat), 65 mg chol, 666 mg sod, 31 g pro, 33 g car, 6 g fiber

EASY ENTERTAINING

Blackened fish with green rice

ACTIVE 20 MIN • **TOTAL** 30 MIN • **SERVES** 4

COST PER SERVING $2.32

1 cup long-grain white rice

2 cups fresh flat-leaf parsley

1 tsp grated lemon zest

3 Tbsp olive oil

Kosher salt and pepper

3 Tbsp paprika

¾ tsp garlic powder

¾ tsp dried thyme

¼ to ½ tsp cayenne

2 Tbsp fresh lemon juice

4 tilapia fillets (about 1½ lb), quartered

Lemon wedges, for serving

❶ Cook the rice according to package directions. Meanwhile, in a food processor, pulse the parsley, lemon zest, 2 Tbsp oil and ¼ tsp each salt and pepper until finely chopped; set aside.

❷ In a small bowl, stir together the paprika, garlic powder, thyme, cayenne, ½ tsp salt and ¼ tsp pepper. Brush the lemon juice over the fish, then coat in the spice mixture.

❸ Heat the remaining Tbsp oil in a large skillet over medium heat. Cook the fish in two batches, adding extra oil if necessary, until the fish begins to blacken and is opaque throughout, 2 to 3 minutes per side.

❹ Fluff the rice with a fork and fold in the parsley mixture. Serve with the fish and lemon wedges, if desired.

♥ **PER SERVING** 478 cal, 15 g fat (3 g sat fat), 77 mg chol, 460 mg sod, 41 g pro, 46 g car, 4 g fiber

Cook's tip » Make a big batch of the spice mixture. Store in an airtight container at room temperature for up to 3 months. Try rubbing it on chicken, steak or pork chops before cooking.

p108

p110

p112

p113

p114

p116

p117

p118

p120

p122

p123

p124

Pasta

p126

p127

p128

FAMILY FAVORITE

Vegetable and three-cheese stuffed shells

ACTIVE 30 MIN • **TOTAL** 45 MIN • **SERVES** 4
COST PER SERVING $3.61

16	jumbo shells (from a 12-oz box)
2	cups marinara sauce
1	10-oz pkg frozen leaf spinach, thawed
½	16-oz pkg frozen broccoli florets, thawed
1	15-oz container part-skim ricotta
2	oz Parmesan, grated (about ½ cup)
4	oz part-skim mozzarella, grated (about 1 cup)
	Kosher salt and pepper
2	Tbsp olive oil
1	Tbsp red wine vinegar
1	small head romaine lettuce, torn
1	seedless cucumber, thinly sliced
½	small red onion, thinly sliced

1 Heat oven to 400°F. Cook the pasta according to package directions. Drain and rinse under cold water to cool.

2 Spread the sauce onto the bottom of a large broiler-proof baking dish.

3 Squeeze the spinach of excess moisture, roughly chop and place in a large bowl. Chop the broccoli and add it to the bowl. Stir in the ricotta, Parmesan, ½ cup of the mozzarella and ½ tsp each salt and pepper. Spoon the mixture into the shells (about ¼ cup each) and place on top of the sauce.

4 Sprinkle with the remaining ½ cup mozzarella and bake until the shells are heated through, 10 to 12 minutes. Increase heat to broil. Broil the shells until the cheese begins to brown, 2 to 3 minutes.

5 Meanwhile, in a large bowl, whisk together the oil, vinegar and ¼ tsp each salt and pepper. Toss with the lettuce, cucumber and onion. Serve with the shells.

PER SERVING 676 cal, 29 g fat (11 g sat fat), 48 mg chol, 1,434 mg sod, 38 g pro, 65 g car, 11 g fiber

Make ahead » Prepare the shells, but do not bake. Refrigerate for up to 2 days. When ready to serve, bake at 375°F until heated through, then broil until golden brown.

20-MINUTE MEAL

Linguine and clam sauce

ACTIVE 20 MIN • **TOTAL** 20 MIN • **SERVES** 4
COST PER SERVING $2.74

12	oz linguine
2	Tbsp olive oil
3	cloves garlic, thinly sliced
1	cup dry white wine
2	beefsteak tomatoes, chopped
¼	tsp crushed red pepper flakes
	Kosher salt
20	littleneck or Manila clams, rinsed
¼	cup fresh flat-leaf parsley, roughly chopped
	Crusty bread, for serving

1 Cook the linguine according to package directions; drain and return it to the pot.

2 Meanwhile, heat the oil in a large skillet over medium heat. Add the garlic and cook, stirring, until it begins to brown, 1 minute. Add the wine, tomatoes, crushed red pepper and ½ tsp salt, and bring to a boil.

3 Add the clams and simmer, covered, until they open, 4 to 6 minutes. Toss the linguine with the clam sauce and parsley. Serve with bread, if desired.

♥ **PER SERVING** 464 cal, 9 g fat (1 g sat fat), 22 mg chol, 694 mg sod, 24 g pro, 72 g car, 4 g fiber

Prep tip » Select clams with tightly closed shells free of breaks, chips or cracks. To keep them fresh, refrigerate them in a bowl for up to 2 days (sealing them in a plastic bag or immersing them in water will cause them to die).

Rigatoni with roasted broccoli and red onions

ACTIVE 15 MIN • **TOTAL** 30 MIN • **SERVES** 4
COST PER SERVING $1.66

4	cloves garlic, smashed
1	head broccoli, cut into small florets
1	large red onion, cut into ½-in.-thick wedges
2	Tbsp olive oil
	Kosher salt and pepper
4	slices bacon
12	oz rigatoni
½	cup grated Parmesan (2 oz)

* We consider olive oil, salt and pepper to be staples, so they
  are not included in the ingredient count for this recipe.

Top it off » Add a little zip to this dish with a dash of bright lemon flavor. Use a vegetable peeler to remove strips of zest, and then thinly slice them. Add to the pasta when adding the Parmesan, along with 1 Tbsp fresh lemon juice.

❶ Position racks to divide the oven in thirds. Heat oven to 425°F. On a large rimmed baking sheet, toss the garlic, broccoli, onion, oil and ¼ tsp each salt and pepper and roast on the lower rack until golden brown and tender, 20 to 25 minutes.

❷ Arrange the bacon on a second rimmed baking sheet and roast (on the upper rack above the vegetables) until crisp, 12 to 15 minutes. Transfer to a paper towel–lined plate. Break into pieces when cool.

❸ Meanwhile, cook the pasta according to package directions. Reserve ¾ cup of the cooking water, drain the pasta and return it to the pot. Add ½ cup of the reserved cooking liquid, sprinkle with ¼ cup Parmesan and toss to coat (add more cooking liquid if the pasta seems dry).

❹ Add the roasted vegetable mixture and bacon to the pasta and toss to combine. Serve with the remaining Parmesan.

♥ **PER SERVING** 511 cal, 16 g fat (5 g sat fat), 21 mg chol, 547 mg sod, 23 g pro, 72 g car, 6 g fiber

SLOW COOKER

Pork ragu

ACTIVE 20 MIN • **TOTAL** 5 HR 20 MIN OR 8 HR 20 MIN • **SERVES** 4
COST PER SERVING $3.01

1	28-oz can whole tomatoes, drained
4	cloves garlic, finely chopped
2	medium carrots, cut into ¼-in. pieces
1	large onion, chopped
½	cup dry white wine
2	tsp dried oregano
	Kosher salt and pepper
2½	lb pork shoulder, trimmed and quartered
12	oz pappardelle or other wide noodle
½	cup fresh flat-leaf parsley, chopped
¼	cup grated Parmesan (1 oz)

1 In a 5- to 6-qt slow cooker, combine the tomatoes, garlic, carrots, onion, wine, oregano and ½ tsp each salt and pepper.

2 Add the pork to the slow cooker and cook, covered, until the pork is cooked through and easily pulls apart, 6 to 8 hours on low or 4 to 5 hours on high.

3 Twenty minutes before serving, cook the pasta according to package directions. Using a fork, break the meat into smaller pieces, then stir it into the cooking liquid; fold in the parsley. Serve the pork over the pasta and sprinkle with the Parmesan.

PER SERVING 650 cal, 14 g fat (5 g sat fat), 118 mg chol, 761 mg sod, 51 g pro, 78 g car, 6 g fiber

Make ahead » Prepare the ragu, but do not make the pasta. Freeze the ragu in an airtight container for up to 3 months. Thaw in the refrigerator overnight. Reheat in a large saucepan, covered, over medium heat, until warm, about 10 minutes (if ragu starts to dry out, add ¼ to ½ cup water or chicken broth).

5-INGREDIENT MEAL*

Ravioli with sautéed asparagus and walnuts

ACTIVE 20 MIN • **TOTAL** 20 MIN • **SERVES** 4

COST PER SERVING $2.25

1	14- to 16-oz pkg cheese ravioli (fresh or frozen)
¼	cup olive oil
2	cloves garlic, thinly sliced
½	cup walnuts, roughly chopped
8	oz asparagus, trimmed and thinly sliced on a diagonal
	Kosher salt and pepper
¼	cup grated Parmesan (1 oz)

* We consider olive oil, salt and pepper to be staples, so they are not included in the ingredient count for this recipe.

1 Cook the ravioli according to package directions.

2 Meanwhile, heat the oil in a medium skillet over medium heat. Add the garlic and walnuts and cook, stirring often, until the nuts are lightly toasted and fragrant and the garlic is golden brown, 3 to 5 minutes.

3 Add the asparagus, season with ¼ tsp each salt and pepper and cook, tossing occasionally, until just tender, about 2 minutes. Serve over the ravioli and sprinkle with the Parmesan.

PER SERVING 417 cal, 26 g fat (5 g sat fat), 16 mg chol, 265 mg sod, 13 g pro, 32 g car, 3 g fiber

Love your leftovers » Transform the leftover asparagus-walnut mixture into an easy hors d'oeuvre by mixing in the Parmesan (or substituting feta cheese) and spooning it on top of crostini, crackers or endive leaves.

Shrimp, cherry pepper and arugula linguine

ACTIVE 15 MIN • **TOTAL** 20 MIN • **SERVES** 4
COST PER SERVING $3.08

12	oz linguine
2	Tbsp olive oil
2	cloves garlic, thinly sliced
¾	cup dry white wine
1	lb peeled and deveined large shrimp
	Kosher salt and pepper
⅓	cup small sweet red cherry peppers (such as Peppadew), quartered
4	cups baby arugula

1 Cook the linguine according to package directions. Reserve ¼ cup of the cooking liquid; drain the pasta and return it to the pot.

2 Meanwhile, heat the oil in a large skillet over medium heat. Add the garlic and cook, stirring, until light golden brown, about 1 minute. Add the wine and bring to a simmer.

3 Season the shrimp with ¼ tsp each salt and pepper, add to the skillet along with the cherry peppers and cook, turning the shrimp once, until they are opaque throughout, about 2 minutes per side.

4 Toss the pasta with the shrimp mixture and arugula (add the reserved cooking liquid, 1 Tbsp at a time, if the pasta seems dry).

PER SERVING 473 cal, 9 g fat (1 g sat fat), 143 mg chol, 796 mg sod, 28 g pro, 69 g car, 3 g fiber

Use up the cherry peppers » Make an easy spread for crackers: Chop the sweet, slightly hot peppers and mix them with cream cheese and chopped parsley. Or fold them into steamed rice, tuna salad or scrambled eggs.

5-INGREDIENT MEAL*

Pasta with roasted cauliflower, tomatoes and pepperoni

ACTIVE 15 MIN • **TOTAL** 30 MIN • **SERVES** 4
COST PER SERVING $1.90

1	small head cauliflower (about 1½ lb), cored and sliced ¼ in. thick
2	Tbsp olive oil
	Kosher salt and pepper
12	oz medium shells or other short pasta
1	pint small grape tomatoes
3	oz pepperoni, very thinly sliced
½	cup fresh flat-leaf parsley, chopped

* We consider olive oil, salt and pepper to be staples, so they are not included in the ingredient count for this recipe.

❶ Heat oven to 425°F. On a large rimmed baking sheet, toss the cauliflower, oil, ½ tsp salt and ¼ tsp pepper. Roast for 12 minutes.

❷ Meanwhile, cook the pasta according to package directions. Drain the pasta and return it to the pot.

❸ Add the tomatoes to the cauliflower, toss to combine and roast for 6 minutes more. Scatter the pepperoni over the vegetables and roast until the cauliflower is golden brown and tender, 6 to 8 minutes more. Toss the pasta with the cauliflower mixture and parsley.

PER SERVING 507 cal, 18 g fat (5 g sat fat), 22 mg chol, 624 mg sod, 19 g pro, 70 g car, 5 g fiber

Love your leftovers » Scatter the cauliflower mixture over pizza dough. Top with cheese and bake per package directions.

6-INGREDIENT MEAL*

Brown butter tortellini with toasted garlic and asparagus

ACTIVE 20 MIN • **TOTAL** 20 MIN • **SERVES** 4
COST PER SERVING $1.25

1	lb cheese tortellini
1	lemon
3	Tbsp unsalted butter
8	oz thin asparagus, thinly sliced on a diagonal
2	cloves garlic, finely chopped
	Kosher salt and pepper
2	Tbsp fresh tarragon, chopped
	Grated Parmesan, for serving

* We consider salt and pepper to be staples, so they are not included in the ingredient count for this recipe.

❶ Cook the tortellini according to package directions. Drain.

❷ Meanwhile, using a vegetable peeler, remove 3 strips of zest from the lemon. Thinly slice the zest.

❸ Melt the butter in a large skillet over medium heat. Add the asparagus and garlic, season with ¼ tsp each salt and pepper and cook, tossing occasionally, until beginning to soften, 2 to 3 minutes. Increase the heat to medium-high, add the lemon zest and cook, tossing, until the butter turns golden brown, about 2 minutes.

❹ Toss the asparagus mixture with the tortellini and tarragon. Serve with Parmesan, if desired.

PER SERVING 442 cal, 19 g fat (10 g sat fat), 72 mg chol, 543 mg sod, 17 g pro, 55 g car, 4 g fiber

Use up the tarragon » Roughly chop the leftover tarragon and fold into scrambled eggs, toss with boiled potatoes and olive oil, whisk into creamy salad dressings or throw into a green salad.

5-INGREDIENT MEAL*

Spaghetti with bacon, eggs and Swiss chard

ACTIVE 20 MIN • **TOTAL** 20 MIN • **SERVES** 4

COST PER SERVING $1.33

12	oz spaghetti
1	small bunch Swiss chard, stems discarded and leaves cut into 1-in. strips
8	slices bacon
1	tsp olive oil
4	large eggs
½	cup grated Parmesan (2 oz), plus more for serving
	Kosher salt and pepper

* We consider olive oil, salt and pepper to be staples, so they are not included in the ingredient count for this recipe.

❶ Cook the pasta according to package directions, adding the chard during the last 3 minutes of cooking. Reserve ½ cup of the cooking water, drain the pasta and chard and return them to the pot.

❷ Meanwhile, cook the bacon in a large nonstick skillet over medium heat until crisp, 6 to 8 minutes. Transfer to a paper towel-lined plate. Break into pieces when cool.

❸ Wipe out the skillet and heat the oil over medium heat. Crack the eggs into the skillet and cook to desired doneness, 3 to 4 minutes for runny yolks.

❹ Toss the pasta and chard with the reserved pasta water, Parmesan, ½ tsp salt and ¼ tsp pepper; fold in the bacon. Divide among bowls and top with the eggs. Season the eggs with salt and pepper and sprinkle with additional Parmesan, if desired.

PER SERVING 548 cal, 17 g fat (6 g sat fat), 212 mg chol, 910 mg sod, 29 g pro, 67 g car, 5 g fiber

Prep tip » In general, the smaller the chard leaf the sweeter it will taste. Look for bunches with stalks that feel firm and crisp and leaves without blemishes or holes.

Switch it up »
For a twist, try spinach tortellini, mushroom ravioli or butternut squash agnolotti.

5-INGREDIENT MEAL*

Ravioli with sausage and Brussels sprouts

ACTIVE 20 MIN • **TOTAL** 20 MIN • **SERVES** 4

COST PER SERVING $2.46

1	lb cheese ravioli
2	Tbsp olive oil
½	lb Italian turkey sausage, casings removed
12	oz Brussels sprouts, trimmed and thinly sliced
	Kosher salt and pepper
½	cup low-sodium chicken broth
¼	cup grated Parmesan or Romano cheese (1 oz)

❶ Cook the ravioli according to package directions.

❷ Meanwhile, heat the oil in a large skillet over medium-high heat. Add the sausage and cook, breaking it up with a spoon, until browned, 6 to 7 minutes.

❸ Add the Brussels sprouts, ½ tsp salt and ¼ tsp pepper and cook, tossing, for 2 minutes. Add the chicken broth and bring to a simmer. Serve over the ravioli and sprinkle with cheese, if desired.

PER SERVING 413 cal, 21 g fat (8 g sat fat), 60 mg chol, 938 mg sod, 24 g pro, 34 g car, 4 g fiber

* We consider olive oil, salt and pepper to be staples, so they are not included in the ingredient count for this recipe.

20-MINUTE MEAL

Spaghetti with roasted zucchini

ACTIVE 10 MIN • **TOTAL** 20 MIN • **SERVES** 4

COST PER SERVING 78¢

- 12 oz spaghetti
- 3 Tbsp olive oil
- 2 ½-in.-thick slices fresh bread, torn into 1-in. pieces
- 2 cloves garlic, smashed
- 4 small zucchini (about 1 lb total), sliced ¼ in. thick
- ¼ to ½ tsp crushed red pepper flakes
  Kosher salt
- ¼ cup grated Parmesan (1 oz)
- ¼ cup fresh flat-leaf parsley, chopped
- 1 Tbsp grated lemon zest

1 Heat oven to 425°F. Cook the pasta according to package directions. Drain the pasta and return it to the pot; toss with 1 Tbsp oil.

2 Meanwhile, in a food processor, pulse the bread and garlic until the bread forms coarse crumbs and the garlic is chopped.

3 In a large bowl, toss the zucchini, crushed red pepper, remaining 2 Tbsp oil and ½ tsp salt. Add the Parmesan and bread crumb mixture and toss to combine.

4 Spread the zucchini mixture on 2 rimmed baking sheets and roast until the zucchini is tender and golden brown, 10 to 12 minutes. Toss the pasta with the zucchini mixture, parsley and lemon zest.

Switch it up » For a one-pan meal, skip the pasta and toss 1 lb large raw peeled and deveined shrimp with the zucchini and bread crumb mixture before roasting.

♥ **PER SERVING** 496 cal, 14 g fat (3 g sat fat), 4 mg chol, 448 mg sod, 16 g pro, 76 g car, 6 g fiber

Winter squash lasagna

ACTIVE 15 MIN • **TOTAL** 35 MIN • **SERVES** 4

COST PER SERVING $1.88

1	15-oz container part-skim ricotta
4	oz part-skim mozzarella, coarsely grated
⅛	tsp freshly grated or ground nutmeg
¼	cup plus 2 Tbsp grated Parmesan
	Kosher salt and pepper
1	bunch spinach, thick stems discarded, leaves chopped
1	12-oz pkg frozen winter squash purée, thawed
6	no-boil lasagna noodles
	Green salad, for serving

❶ Heat oven to 425°F. In a large bowl, combine the ricotta, mozzarella, nutmeg, ¼ cup Parmesan, ½ tsp salt and ¼ tsp pepper; fold in the spinach.

❷ Spread ½ cup of the squash on the bottom of an 8-in. square baking dish. Top with 2 noodles and spread a third (about ¼ cup) of the remaining squash over the top. Dollop with a third (about 1 cup) of the ricotta mixture; repeat. Place the remaining 2 noodles on top; spread with the remaining squash and dollop with the remaining ricotta mixture.

❸ Sprinkle with the remaining 2 Tbsp Parmesan, cover tightly with an oiled piece of foil (to prevent sticking) and bake for 15 minutes. Uncover and bake until the noodles are tender and the top is golden brown, 8 to 10 minutes.

PER SERVING 433 cal, 17 g fat (8 g sat fat), 50 mg chol, 664 mg sod, 28 g pro, 41 g car, 4 g fiber

Make ahead » Refrigerate the cooked lasagna for up to 3 days or freeze for up to 2 months. Thaw in the refrigerator overnight, if frozen. Bake, covered, at 375°F until heated through.

Pasta with quick meat sauce

ACTIVE 25 MIN • **TOTAL** 25 MIN • **SERVES** 4
COST PER SERVING $1.99

12	oz fettuccine or any long pasta
2	Tbsp olive oil
1	large onion, chopped
	Kosher salt and pepper
1	medium carrot, finely diced
1	stalk celery, finely diced
2	large cloves garlic, finely chopped

¾	lb lean ground beef
¼	cup dry white wine
¼	to ½ tsp crushed red pepper flakes
⅛	tsp ground cinnamon
⅛	tsp freshly grated or ground nutmeg
1	28-oz can crushed tomatoes
¾	cup fresh flat-leaf parsley, chopped

> *Make ahead »* Refrigerate the meat sauce for up to 3 days or freeze for up to 3 months. Thaw in the refrigerator overnight, if frozen. Reheat in a medium saucepan, covered, stirring occasionally (add ½ cup water if sauce is too thick or drying out). Cook the pasta just before serving.

❶ Cook the pasta according to package directions.

❷ Meanwhile, heat the oil in a large skillet over medium heat. Add the onion, season with ½ tsp each salt and pepper and cook, covered, stirring occasionally, for 5 minutes. Add the carrot, celery and garlic and cook, covered, stirring occasionally, until they begin to soften, about 4 minutes more.

❸ While the vegetables cook, combine the beef and wine in a medium bowl; break up the beef with a spoon.

❹ Add the beef mixture to the vegetables, increase the heat to medium-high and cook, breaking it up with a spoon, until the liquid has evaporated and the meat begins to brown, about 3 minutes. Stir in the crushed red pepper, cinnamon and nutmeg.

❺ Add the tomatoes to the skillet and simmer until the mixture is slightly thickened, about 3 minutes. Stir in the parsley and toss with the pasta.

PER SERVING 596 cal, 17 g fat (5 g sat fat), 55 mg chol, 767 mg sod, 31 g pro, 79 g car, 6 g fiber

FAMILY FAVORITE

Creamy pasta with leeks, peas and Parmesan

ACTIVE 25 MIN • **TOTAL** 25 MIN • **SERVES** 4
COST PER SERVING $2.25

12	oz orecchiette pasta
1	10-oz pkg frozen peas
1	lemon
2	Tbsp olive oil
4	leeks (white and light green parts only), cut into ¼-in.-thick half-moons
	Kosher salt and pepper
¾	cup heavy cream
⅛	tsp freshly grated nutmeg (optional)
2	Tbsp fresh tarragon, chopped
¼	cup grated Parmesan (1 oz)

❶ Cook the pasta according to package directions, adding the peas during the last 2 minutes of cooking; drain.

❷ Meanwhile, using a vegetable peeler, remove 4 strips of zest from the lemon and thinly slice on a diagonal.

❸ Heat the oil in a large skillet over medium heat. Add the leeks, ½ tsp salt and ¼ tsp pepper and cook, stirring occasionally, until tender, 6 to 8 minutes. Add the cream, lemon zest and nutmeg (if using) and simmer until slightly thickened, 2 to 3 minutes.

❹ Add the pasta and peas to the skillet and toss to combine; fold in the tarragon. Sprinkle with the Parmesan before serving.

Prep tip » To thoroughly clean leeks, place the cut pieces into a bowl of cold water, swish them around, and lift them out with a slotted spoon, leaving the grit behind in the water. Drain and repeat until the water is clear.

PER SERVING 643 cal, 25 g fat (11 g sat fat), 64 mg chol, 435 mg sod, 19 g pro, 88 g car, 8 g fiber

FAMILY FAVORITE

Cheesy shells and greens

ACTIVE 20 MIN • **TOTAL** 30 MIN • **SERVES** 4
COST PER SERVING $1.31

12	oz medium pasta shells
1	Tbsp unsalted butter
2	Tbsp all-purpose flour
1¼	cups whole milk
1	Tbsp Dijon mustard
½	freshly grated or ground nutmeg
	Pinch cayenne (optional)
6	oz extra-sharp Cheddar, grated (1½ cups)
	Kosher salt and pepper
1	bunch spinach, thick stems discarded, leaves roughly chopped

➊ Cook the pasta according to the package directions.

➋ Meanwhile, melt the butter in a large pot over medium heat. Add the flour and cook, stirring, for 2 minutes; whisk in the milk. Cook, stirring occasionally, until slightly thickened, 5 minutes.

➌ Whisk in the mustard, nutmeg, cayenne (if using), 1 cup Cheddar, ½ tsp salt and ¼ tsp pepper. Add the pasta and spinach and toss to combine.

➍ Heat broiler. Transfer the mixture to a 1½-qt broiler-proof baking dish or four 12-oz ramekins. Sprinkle with the remaining ½ cup Cheddar and broil until golden brown, 3 to 4 minutes.

PER SERVING 593 cal, 22 g fat (14 g sat fat), 61 mg chol, 677 mg sod, 25 g pro, 73 g car, 4 g fiber

Top it off » Add a crispy bread crumb topping to this dish: Pulse 4 slices of bread in a food processor to form coarse crumbs. Stir in ¼ cup finely chopped fresh flat-leaf parsley and 2 Tbsp olive oil. Sprinkle over the pasta before broiling.

p145

p146

p148

Vegetarian

p149

p150

p152

ONE-POT

Butternut squash risotto

ACTIVE 35 MIN • **TOTAL** 35 MIN • **SERVES** 4
COST PER SERVING $1.22

2	Tbsp olive oil
1	medium onion, finely chopped
½	medium butternut squash (about 1 lb), peeled and cut into ¼-in. pieces
2	cloves garlic, finely chopped
	Kosher salt and pepper
¾	cup Arborio rice
1	cup dry white wine
3½	cups low-sodium vegetable broth
2	tsp fresh thyme
¼	cup grated Romano cheese or Parmesan (1 oz), plus more for serving

❶ Heat the oil in a large skillet over medium heat. Add the onion and cook, covered, stirring occasionally, until tender, 6 to 8 minutes.

❷ Add the butternut squash, garlic, ½ tsp salt and ¼ tsp pepper and cook, covered, stirring occasionally, until the squash begins to soften, 5 to 6 minutes. Stir in the rice and cook for 1 minute.

❸ Add the wine and simmer until absorbed, 6 to 10 minutes. Add the broth and simmer, stirring occasionally, until the rice is tender and creamy and the broth has been absorbed, 18 to 20 minutes.

❹ Stir in the thyme and Romano. Serve with additional Romano, if desired.

♥ **PER SERVING** 306 cal, 10 g fat (3 g sat fat), 14 mg chol, 504 mg sod, 10 g pro, 44 g car, 3 g fiber

Love your leftovers » For a delicious appetizer, make risotto balls. In a medium bowl, combine 2 cups leftover risotto with 1 large egg and ¼ cup grated Romano cheese or Parmesan. With wet hands, form the mixture into 3-in. balls. Push a small piece of mozzarella into the center. In a shallow bowl, combine 1 cup panko bread crumbs and 1 Tbsp olive oil. Coat the balls in bread crumbs and place on a parchment-lined baking sheet. Bake at 400°F until lightly golden brown and heated through, 20 to 25 minutes.

5-INGREDIENT MEAL*

Grilled eggplant Parmesan pizza

ACTIVE 25 MIN • **TOTAL** 25 MIN • **SERVES** 4

COST PER SERVING $1.30

1	**lb pizza dough, thawed if frozen**
3	**Tbsp olive oil**
2	**small eggplants (about 1 lb total), sliced ¼ in. thick**
2	**medium tomatoes (about 1 lb total), cut into 1-in. wedges**
	Kosher salt and pepper
½	**cup fresh basil leaves, torn**
½	**cup ricotta**

* We consider olive oil, salt and pepper to be staples, so they are not included in the ingredient count for this recipe.

❶ Heat grill to medium. Shape the pizza dough into two 10-in. rounds. Place on a baking sheet and brush top of each round with 1 tsp of the oil.

❷ Brush the eggplant slices and tomato wedges with 2 Tbsp of the oil and season with ¼ tsp each salt and pepper. Grill the eggplant, covered, until slightly charred and tender, 3 to 4 minutes per side. Grill the tomatoes until slightly charred, about 2 minutes per side. Transfer the vegetables to a plate and cover with foil to keep warm.

❸ Place the pizza dough oiled side down on the grill and cook, covered, until the tops begin to bubble and the bottoms become crisp, about 2 minutes. Brush the tops of the dough with the remaining 2 tsp oil. Turn over and grill until golden brown and crisp, about 2 minutes more.

❹ Transfer the grilled dough back to the baking sheet or to a cutting board. Top with the eggplant, tomatoes and basil. Dollop with the ricotta and sprinkle with pepper, if desired.

♥ **PER SERVING** 459 cal, 17 g fat (4 g sat fat), 16 mg chol, 732 mg sod, 16 g pro, 63 g car, 5 g fiber

Prep tip » Shaping pizza dough can be tricky. If it shrinks back as you stretch it, let it rest for 5 to 10 minutes before trying to shape it again.

Summer minestrone

ACTIVE 30 MIN • **TOTAL** 30 MIN • **SERVES** 4

COST PER SERVING $1.58

1 Tbsp olive oil	1 small zucchini (about 6 oz), cut into ½-in. pieces
1 large onion, finely chopped	1 small yellow squash (about 6 oz), cut into ½-in. pieces
Kosher salt and pepper	
½ small bunch basil (about 2 cups)	1 small carrot, thinly sliced
2 cloves garlic, finely chopped	½ cup frozen peas
	1 cup fresh corn kernels (from 1 ear)
8 oz red potatoes, cut into ½-in. pieces	¼ cup grated Parmesan
4 cups low-sodium vegetable broth	Country bread, for serving

1 Heat the oil in a large heavy-bottomed saucepan over medium heat. Add the onion, season with ½ tsp each salt and pepper and cook, covered, stirring occasionally, for 5 minutes. Uncover and cook, stirring occasionally, until the onions are tender and beginning to brown, 4 to 5 minutes more.

2 Meanwhile, separate the basil leaves from the stems. Finely chop enough stems to yield 1 Tbsp. Add the chopped stems to the onion along with the garlic and cook, stirring, for 1 minute. Add the potatoes and broth and simmer for 5 minutes.

3 Add the zucchini, squash and carrot and simmer for 3 minutes. Add the peas and corn and simmer until the vegetables are just tender, 2 to 3 minutes more. Sprinkle with the Parmesan and basil leaves before serving. Serve with the bread, if desired.

♥ **PER SERVING** 187 cal, 6 g fat (1.5 g sat fat), 0 mg chol, 488 mg sod, 7 g pro, 29 g car, 5 g fiber

Top it off » For an extra burst of flavor, drizzle the soup with store-bought pesto before serving.

UNDER 400 CALORIES

Butternut squash and kale torte

ACTIVE 15 MIN • **TOTAL** 45 MIN • **SERVES** 4

COST PER SERVING $1.66

- 1 Tbsp olive oil, plus more for the pan
- ½ small butternut squash (about 1 lb), thinly sliced
- 1 medium red onion, thinly sliced
- 1 small bunch kale, thick stems discarded and leaves cut into 1-in. pieces

  Kosher salt and pepper
- 1 medium Yukon gold potato (about 6 oz), thinly sliced
- 6 oz thinly sliced provolone cheese (from the deli counter)
- 1 plum tomato, thinly sliced
- ¼ cup grated Parmesan (1 oz)

  Marinara sauce and crusty bread, for serving

Prep tip » To quickly separate kale leaves from the stem, hold the kale in one hand by the stem end, and remove the leaf by pulling it downward.

❶ Heat oven to 425°F. Oil a 9-in. springform pan. Arrange half the butternut squash in the bottom of the pan, in concentric circles. Top with half the onion, separating the rings. Top with half the kale, drizzle with half the oil and season with ¼ tsp salt. Top with the potatoes and half the provolone cheese.

❷ Top with remaining kale, drizzle with the remaining oil and season with ¼ tsp each salt and pepper. Top with the remaining onion, tomato and provolone. Arrange the remaining squash on top and sprinkle with the Parmesan.

❸ Cover with foil, place on a baking sheet and bake for 20 minutes. Remove foil and bake until the vegetables are tender and the top begins to brown, 8 to 10 minutes more. Remove the torte from the pan and cut into pieces. Spoon marinara sauce over the top and serve with the bread, if desired.

PER SERVING 340 cal, 19 g fat (9 g sat fat), 36 mg chol, 754 mg sod, 18 g pro, 28 g car, 5 g fiber

FAMILY FAVORITE

Grilled mushroom and spinach quesadillas

ACTIVE 25 MIN • **TOTAL** 25 MIN • **SERVES** 4
COST PER SERVING $2.84

2   tomatoes, cut into ½-in. pieces
1   avocado, cut into ½-in. pieces
2   Tbsp fresh lemon juice
2   Tbsp olive oil
    Kosher salt and pepper
½   cup fresh cilantro, chopped
4   medium flour tortillas
6   oz Muenster cheese, shredded
4   cups baby spinach
4   medium portobello
    mushroom caps
    Sour cream, for serving

❶ Heat grill to medium. In a medium bowl, combine the tomatoes, avocado, lemon juice, 1 Tbsp oil and ¼ tsp each salt and pepper; fold in the cilantro. Set aside.

❷ Place the tortillas on a large rimmed baking sheet. Divide half the cheese among the tortillas, sprinkling it only on one half. Top that same half with the spinach and remaining cheese.

❸ Place the mushrooms on a cutting board. Brush with the remaining Tbsp oil, season with ½ tsp each salt and pepper and grill, covered, until just tender, 3 to 4 minutes per side. Transfer to the cutting board and thinly slice.

❹ Divide the mushrooms among the tortillas, then fold over tortillas to cover the filling. Grill until the tortillas are crisp and the cheese has melted, about 2 minutes per side. Cut the quesadillas and serve with the tomato-avocado mixture, and sour cream, if desired.

PER SERVING 542 cal, 30 g fat (11 g sat fat), 41 mg chol, 1,124 mg sod, 20 g pro, 49 g car, 8 g fiber

Use up the spinach » Make a quick dip: In a food processor, finely chop 2 scallions (cut into 1-in. pieces) and 2 cups baby spinach. Add 1 cup sour cream, ¼ tsp salt and ⅛ tsp pepper and pulse to combine. Serve with pretzels and vegetables for dipping.

Escarole, red onion, mushroom and egg salad

ACTIVE 25 MIN • **TOTAL** 25 MIN • **SERVES** 4

COST PER SERVING $3.67

4	Tbsp plus 1 tsp olive oil
2	small red onions, sliced into ¼-in.-thick rounds
1	oz mixed mushrooms, sliced
	Kosher salt and pepper
1	Tbsp red wine vinegar
2	tsp Dijon mustard
½	large bunch escarole, torn into bite-size pieces
4	large eggs

❶ Heat 2 Tbsp oil in a large skillet over medium-high heat. Add onions and cook, stirring often, until they begin to soften, 3 to 4 minutes. Add mushrooms, ¼ tsp each salt and pepper, and cook, tossing often, until just tender, about 4 minutes; remove from heat.

❷ In a large bowl, whisk together the vinegar, mustard, 2 Tbsp oil and ⅛ tsp each salt and pepper. Add escarole and toss to coat. Fold in onions and mushrooms.

❸ Heat remaining 1 tsp oil in a large nonstick skillet over medium heat. Crack the eggs into skillet and cook, covered, to desired doneness, 2 to 4 minutes for slightly runny yolks. Serve the eggs with the salad.

Use up the escarole » Heat 2 Tbsp olive oil in a large skillet over medium heat. Add 2 cloves (sliced) and ¼ tsp crushed red pepper and sauté for 1 minute. Add the leftover escarole (torn into 2-in. pieces), season with salt and pepper and sauté until escarole begins to wilt, 2 to 3 minutes. Add 1 cup canned white bean (rinsed) and cook until heated through.

PER SERVING 403 cal, 35 g fat (6 g sat fat), 212 mg chol, 644 mg sod, 12 g pro, 14 g car, 5 g fiber

UNDER 400 CALORIES

Tex-mex gazpacho

ACTIVE 25 MIN • **TOTAL** 25 MIN • **SERVES** 4
COST PER SERVING $1.46

2	jalapeños, seeded
1	cup fresh corn kernels (from 1 ear)
½	cup fresh cilantro, roughly chopped
4	Tbsp fresh lime juice
	Kosher salt and pepper
2	lb tomatoes, quartered
1	seedless cucumber, cut in ½-in. pieces
1	red bell pepper, roughly chopped
½	small sweet onion, roughly chopped
2	Tbsp olive oil
	Warmed flour tortillas, for serving

❶ Finely chop 1 jalapeño. In a medium bowl, combine the jalapeño, corn, cilantro, 1 Tbsp lime juice and ¼ tsp each salt and pepper; set aside.

❷ Roughly chop the remaining jalapeño. Working in batches, purée the jalapeño, tomatoes, cucumber, bell pepper and onion, transferring the puréed mixture to a large bowl. Stir in the oil, remaining 3 Tbsp lime juice, ¾ tsp salt and ¼ tsp pepper. Top with the corn relish and serve with tortillas, if desired.

PER SERVING 160 cal, 8 g fat (1 g sat fat), 0 mg chol, 381 mg sod, 4 g pro, 22 g car, 5 g fiber

Use up the cilantro » Liven up your standard green salad. Cut off and discard the thick stems and toss the rest with torn lettuce or mixed greens before adding your favorite vinaigrette.

UNDER 400 CALORIES

Pierogies and cabbage

ACTIVE 25 MIN • **TOTAL** 25 MIN • **SERVES** 4

COST PER SERVING $1.06

1   16-oz box frozen potato and onion pierogies

1   Tbsp olive oil

1   large red onion, thinly sliced

½   small red cabbage (about 1 lb), cored and shredded

    Kosher salt and pepper

2   Tbsp balsamic vinegar

1   Tbsp whole-grain mustard

2   Tbsp chopped fresh chives (optional)

❶ Cook the pierogies according to package directions.

❷ Meanwhile, heat the oil in a medium skillet over medium heat. Add the onion and cook, covered, stirring occasionally, until tender, 6 to 7 minutes. Add the cabbage, ½ tsp salt and ¾ tsp pepper and cook, stirring occasionally, for 3 minutes.

❸ Add the vinegar and cook, stirring occasionally, until the cabbage is just tender, 4 to 5 minutes more; stir in the mustard and chives (if using). Serve with the pierogies.

♥ **PER SERVING** 243 cal, 6 g fat (1 g sat fat), 5 mg chol, 742 mg sod, 7 g pro, 43 g car, 4 g fiber

Cook's tip » To pan-fry pierogies, boil them according to package directions; drain. Heat 1 tsp olive oil in a nonstick skillet over medium heat and cook the pierogies until golden brown, 2 to 3 minutes per side.

Risotto with scallions, mushrooms and spinach

ACTIVE 25 MIN • **TOTAL** 40 MIN • **SERVES** 4

COST PER SERVING $2.36

4	Tbsp olive oil
1	medium onion, finely chopped
	Kosher salt and pepper
2	cloves garlic, finely chopped
¾	cup Arborio rice
¾	cup dry white wine
3½	cups low-sodium vegetable broth
¼	cup grated Romano cheese, plus more for serving
1	10-oz pkg button mushrooms, quartered
4	cups baby spinach
2	scallions, thinly sliced

Cook's tip » Arborio rice has a high starch content, which gives risotto its rich creaminess. A medium-grain rice will be just as tasty but won't have the same texture.

1 Heat 2 Tbsp oil in a large skillet over medium heat. Add the onion, ½ tsp salt and ¼ tsp pepper and cook, covered, stirring occasionally, until tender, 6 to 8 minutes. Stir in the garlic and cook for 1 minute.

2 Add the rice and cook, stirring, for 1 minute. Add the wine and simmer until absorbed, 3 to 5 minutes. Add the broth and simmer, stirring occasionally, until the rice is tender and creamy and the broth has been absorbed, 18 to 20 minutes. Stir in the Romano.

3 Meanwhile, heat the remaining 2 Tbsp oil in a second large skillet over medium-high heat. Add the mushrooms, season with ¼ tsp each salt and pepper and cook, tossing occasionally, until golden brown and tender, about 5 minutes. Fold the mushrooms into the risotto along with the spinach and scallions. Top with additional Romano, if desired.

♥ **PER SERVING** 327 cal, 15 g fat (3 g sat fat), 4 mg chol, 610 mg sod, 8 g pro, 40 g car, 4 g fiber

EASY ENTERTAINING

Rustic butternut squash tart

ACTIVE 10 MIN • **TOTAL** 35 MIN • **SERVES** 4

COST PER SERVING $1.15

1	medium red onion, thinly sliced into rings and separated
¼	small butternut squash (about ½ lb), peeled, seeded and very thinly sliced
6	sprigs fresh thyme
2	Tbsp olive oil
	Kosher salt and pepper
4	oz extra-sharp Cheddar, grated (1 cup)
1	refrigerated rolled pie crust
1	large egg, beaten
	Green salad, for serving

❶ Heat oven to 400°F. In a large bowl, toss the onion, squash, thyme, oil, ½ tsp salt and ¼ tsp pepper; fold in the Cheddar.

❷ Working on a piece of parchment paper, roll the pie crust into a 14-in. circle. Slide the paper (and crust) onto a baking sheet. Spoon the squash mixture onto the pie crust, leaving a 2-in. border. Fold the border of the crust over the squash mixture.

❸ Brush the crust with the egg. Bake until the crust is golden brown and the vegetables are tender, 20 to 25 minutes. (Cover with foil if the crust is getting dark.) Serve with a salad, if desired.

PER SERVING 438 cal, 32 g fat (13 g sat fat), 63 mg chol, 715 mg sod, 10 g pro, 31 g car, 2 g fiber

Use up the butternut squash » Make an easy side for chicken, pork or steak. Peel, seed and cut the remaining butternut squash into 1½-in. pieces. On a rimmed baking sheet, toss the squash and 4 cloves garlic (smashed) with 6 sprigs fresh thyme, 2 Tbsp olive oil and ½ tsp each salt and pepper. Roast at 400°F until golden brown and tender, 30 to 35 minutes.

UNDER 400 CALORIES

Broccoli and Cheddar soup

ACTIVE 30 MIN • **TOTAL** 30 MIN • **SERVES** 4
COST PER SERVING $1.74

2	½-in.-thick slices of bread, cut into ½-in. pieces
2	Tbsp olive oil
2	stalks celery, chopped
2	cloves garlic, finely chopped
1	large onion, chopped
1	medium russet potato (about 8 oz), cut into ½-in. pieces
1	bunch broccoli (about 1¼ lb), stalks peeled and thinly sliced
	Kosher salt and pepper
1	cup lowfat milk
¼	tsp freshly grated or ground nutmeg
6	oz extra-sharp Cheddar, coarsely grated

1 Heat oven to 400°F. On a rimmed baking sheet, toss the bread with 1 Tbsp oil. Bake until golden brown and crisp, 5 to 7 minutes; set aside.

2 Heat the remaining Tbsp oil in a large saucepan over medium heat. Add the celery, garlic, onion, potato, broccoli stalks, ¾ tsp salt and ¼ tsp pepper and cook, covered, stirring occasionally, until just tender, 5 to 6 minutes.

3 Meanwhile, cut the remaining broccoli into small florets. Add the florets and 3 cups water to the vegetables, cover and bring to a boil. Once boiling, the broccoli should be just tender; if not, simmer 1 to 2 minutes more.

4 Remove from heat and, using a handheld immersion blender (or a standard blender, working in batches and returning to the saucepan), purée the vegetable mixture. Add the milk and nutmeg and simmer until heated through, about 2 minutes. Add the cheese and stir until melted. Serve with the croutons.

PER SERVING 398 cal, 21 g fat (8 g sat fat), 48 mg chol, 861 mg sod, 17 g pro, 35 g car, 5 g fiber

Make ahead » Prepare the soup (without the cheese) and croutons. Refrigerate the soup and store the croutons at room temperature for up to 3 days. When ready to serve, bring the soup to a simmer in a large saucepan. Add the cheese and stir until melted. Serve with the croutons.

Potato, red onion and kale pizza

ACTIVE 10 MIN • **TOTAL** 35 MIN • **SERVES** 4
COST PER SERVING $1.32

Cornmeal, for the baking sheet

1   lb pizza dough, thawed if frozen

2   medium Yukon gold or white potatoes (about 8 oz), thinly sliced

1   small red onion, thinly sliced

½   bunch kale, thick stems discarded, leaves torn into 2-in. pieces

3   Tbsp olive oil

Kosher salt and pepper

6   oz thinly sliced provolone

❶ Heat oven to 425°F. Dust a baking sheet with cornmeal. Shape the dough into a 16-in. oval or circle and place on the prepared baking sheet.

❷ In a large bowl, toss the potatoes, onion, kale, oil and ½ tsp each salt and pepper. Scatter the vegetables and cheese over the dough and bake until the potatoes are tender and the crust is golden brown and crisp, 20 to 25 minutes.

PER SERVING 604 cal, 24 g fat (9 g sat fat), 29 mg chol, 1,224 mg sod, 25 g pro, 73 g car, 2 g fiber

> *Make ahead »* Refrigerate the cooked pizza for up to 2 days. When ready to serve, bake at 375°F until heated through.

SLOW COOKER

Butternut squash stew

ACTIVE 10 MIN • **TOTAL** 5 HR 10 MIN OR 7 HR 10 MIN • **SERVES** 4
COST PER SERVING $1.95

1	28-oz can whole tomatoes
½	cup raisins
2	tsp ground cumin
1½	tsp ground ginger
¼	tsp ground cinnamon
	Kosher salt and pepper
1	medium red onion, cut into ½-in. wedges
½	medium butternut squash (about 1 lb), peeled, seeded and cut into 1-in. pieces
1	cup couscous
¼	cup fresh cilantro, chopped
1	15-oz can chickpeas, rinsed

Prep tip » To prepare the squash, slice ½ in. off each end, then cut crosswise where the bulb meets the neck. Use a peeler to remove the skin. Cut the bulb in half and scoop out the seeds. Cut as desired.

❶ Place the tomatoes (and their juices) in a 5- to 6-qt slow cooker and break them up slightly. Add the raisins, cumin, ginger, cinnamon, ½ tsp salt and ¼ tsp pepper and mix to combine.

❷ Add the onion and squash and cook, covered, until squash is tender, 5 to 7 hours on low or 3 to 5 hours on high.

❸ Ten minutes before serving, cook the couscous according to package directions; fold in the cilantro. Gently fold the chickpeas into the stew and cook, covered, until heated through, about 3 minutes. Serve over the couscous.

PER SERVING 397 cal, 2.5 g fat (0 g sat fat), 0 mg chol, 873 mg sod, 14 g pro, 86 g car, 14 g fiber

FAMILY FAVORITE

Mexican black bean lasagna

ACTIVE 25 MIN • **TOTAL** 45 MIN • **SERVES** 6
COST PER SERVING $1.47

2	Tbsp olive oil
1	large onion, chopped
2	jalapeños (seeded if desired), finely chopped
1	red bell pepper, cut into ¼-in. pieces
2	cloves garlic, finely chopped
1	15-oz can black beans, rinsed
1	cup frozen corn kernels, thawed
2	tsp chili powder
2	Tbsp fresh lime juice, plus wedges for serving
½	cup fresh cilantro, chopped, plus more for serving
1	10-oz can red enchilada sauce (about 1 cup)
9	small corn tortillas
6	oz Muenster cheese, shredded (about 1½ cups)
	Sour cream and hot sauce, for serving

❶ Heat oven to 425°F. Heat the oil in a large skillet over medium heat. Add the onion and cook, covered, stirring occasionally, for 5 minutes. Add the jalapeños, bell pepper and garlic and cook, covered, stirring occasionally, until the vegetables are just tender, 6 to 8 minutes. Stir in the beans, corn and chili powder and cook for 2 minutes. Remove from heat and stir in the lime juice and cilantro.

❷ Spread ¼ cup enchilada sauce on the bottom of an 8-in. square or 1½ qt baking dish. Top with 3 tortillas, tearing them to fit as necessary. Spread a third of the remaining enchilada sauce over the top (about ¼ cup). Top with a third of the bean mixture and ½ cup cheese; repeat twice.

❸ Bake until the lasagna is heated through and the top begins to brown, 12 to 15 minutes. Let stand for 5 minutes. Serve with sour cream, cilantro, lime wedges and hot sauce, if desired.

- -

PER SERVING 307 cal, 15 g fat (6 g sat fat), 27 mg chol, 654 mg sod, 15 g pro, 34 g car, 8 g fiber

Make ahead » Prepare the lasagna but do not bake. Refrigerate for up to 3 days. When ready to serve, bake at 375°F until heated through and the top begins to brown.

EASY ENTERTAINING

Grilled vegetable salad with couscous and herb pesto

ACTIVE 35 MIN • **TOTAL** 35 MIN • **SERVES** 4
COST PER SERVING $2.69

1	cup couscous
2	cups fresh flat-leaf parsley
1	cup fresh mint leaves
1	Tbsp fresh lemon juice
5	Tbsp olive oil
	Kosher salt and pepper
4	oz feta cheese, crumbled (about 1 cup), plus more for serving
2	small zucchini (about 12 oz), halved lengthwise
1	ear corn, shucked
2	medium portobello mushroom caps (about 6 oz total)
1	red pepper, seeded and quartered
4	scallions
1	15.5-oz can chickpeas, rinsed
2	cups baby spinach

1 Heat grill to medium-high. Prepare the couscous according to package directions.

2 Meanwhile, make the dressing: In a food processor, pulse the parsley and mint until chopped. Add the lemon juice, 3 Tbsp oil, 2 Tbsp water and ½ tsp pepper and pulse to combine. Add the feta and process until nearly smooth.

3 Brush the zucchini, corn, mushrooms, red pepper and scallions with the remaining 2 Tbsp oil; season with ½ tsp each salt and pepper. Grill the vegetables until just tender and slightly charred, 2 to 3 minutes per side. Transfer the vegetables to a cutting board and cut into ½-in. pieces (cut the corn off the cob).

4 Fluff the couscous with a fork and fold in the vegetables and chickpeas. Divide the spinach and couscous mixture among plates. Drizzle with the dressing and sprinkle with additional feta, if desired.

PER SERVING 547 cal, 24 g fat (6 g sat fat), 20 mg chol, 746 mg sod, 20 g pro, 66 g car, 11 g fiber

Switch it up » Take this salad to go. Cut a piece of pita bread in half. Spread with the dressing and stuff with the spinach and salad.

MEASUREMENT CONVERSION CHART

pinch/dash	⅟₁₆ teaspoon		
1 teaspoon			
½ Tablespoon	1½ teaspoons	¼ fl oz	7.5 ml
1 Tablespoon	3 teaspoons	½ fl oz	15 ml
¼ cup	4 Tablespoons	2 fl oz	60 ml
⅓ cup	5 Tablespoons + 1 teaspoon	2½ fl oz	75 ml
½ cup	8 Tablespoons	4 fl oz	120 ml
⅔ cup	10 Tablespoons + 2 teaspoons	5 fl oz	150 ml
¾ cup	12 Tablespoons	6 fl oz	180 ml
1 cup	16 Tablespoons or ½ pint	8 fl oz	240 ml
1 pint	2 cups	16 fl oz	475 ml
1 quart	2 pints or 4 cups	32 fl oz	945 ml
1 gallon	4 quarts or 16 cups	128 fl oz	3.8 liters
1 pound	16 ounces		

WHEN IS IT DONE?

The most accurate way to tell when meat and poultry are done is to use an instant-read thermometer. To the right lists the *Woman's Day* test kitchen's preference (and considered safe by many food experts and chefs) for tender and juicy results.

* The U.S. Department of Agriculture recommends cooking beef, pork and lamb to a minimum internal temperature of 145°F and poultry to 165°F for maximum food safety.

BEEF	WD TEST KITCHEN
Rare	118°F*
Medium-rare	125°F–130°F*
Medium	135°F–140°F*
Medium-well	150°F
Well-done	155°F
LAMB	
Medium-rare	125°F–130°F*
Medium	140°F*
Medium-well	150°F
Well-done	155°F
PORK	145°F
POULTRY	
White Meat	160°F*
Dark Meat	165°F

TEMPERATURE CONVERSION CHART

°F	°C
225°F	110°C
250°F	125°C
275°F	135°C
300°F	150°C
325°F	160°C
350°F	175°C
375°F	190°C
400°F	200°C
425°F	220°C
450°F	230°C

INDEX BY CATEGORY

ACKNOWLEDGEMENTS

There are so many steps that go into producing the recipes you see in these pages and so many people who are integral to their success.

Special thanks to the those who worked together to come up with ideas and develop recipes. And to those who joined us in the test kitchen tweaking and adjusting to ensure each recipe's ease and deliciousness: Anna Helm Baxter, Mimi Freud, Donna Meadow, Yasmin Sabir, Hadas Smirnoff, Chelsea Zimmer.

Thank you to the teams that came together for photo shoots. Along with photographers, these food stylists, prop stylists and art directors help make our food look as good as it tastes: Isabel Abdai, Simon Andrews, Alison Attenborough, Stephana Bottom, Philippa Brathwaite, Cindy Diprima, Molly Fitzsimons, Matthew Gleason, Victoria Granof, Paige Hicks, Vivian Lui, Marina Malchin, Cyd McDowell, Frank Mentesana, Pam Morris, Elizabeth Press, Maggie Ruggiero, Pamela Duncan Silver, Susan Spungen, Susan Sugarman, Erin Swift, Victor Thompson, Alistair Turnbull, Gerri Williams, Sara Williams, Amy Wilson, Michelle Wong.

HEARST BOOKS
New York

An Imprint of Sterling Publishing
387 Park Avenue South
New York, NY 10016

....

Editor-in-Chief Susan Spencer
Creative Director Sara Williams
Deputy Creative Director Victor Thompson
Executive Editor Annemarie Conte
Food & Nutrition Director Kate Merker
Senior Associate Food Editor Yasmin Sabir
Associate Food Editor Anna Helm Baxter
Copy Editor Lauren Spencer
Food Intern Hallie Milano

....

ISBN 978-1-61837-124-9

Library of Congress Cataloging-in-Publication Data

Woman's day easy everyday dinners : go-to family recipes for each night of the week.
    pages cm
  Includes index.
  ISBN 978-1-61837-124-9
1. Quick and easy cooking. 2. Dinners and dining. I. Woman's day. II. Title: Easy everyday dinners.
TX833.5.W66 2013
641.5'55--dc23
                        2013018823

Distributed in Canada by Sterling Publishing
C/o Canadian Manda Group, 165 Dufferin Street
Toronto, Ontario, Canada M6K 3H6
Distributed in the United Kingdom by GMC Distribution Services
Castle Place, 166 High Street, Lewes, East Sussex, England BN7 1XU
Distributed in Australia by Capricorn Link (Australia) Pty. Ltd.
P.O. Box 704, Windsor, NSW 2756, Australia

For information about custom editions, special sales, and premium and corporate purchases, please contact Sterling Special Sales at 800-805-5489 or specialsales@sterlingpublishing.com.

Manufactured in Canada

2 4 6 8 10 9 7 5 3 1

www.sterlingpublishing.com